Spiritual Food For Thought

100 Brief Reflections on Living The Christian Faith In A Busy World

By
James J. Walsh

NIHIL OBSTAT
Rev. John R. Roos
Censor Librorum

IMPRIMATUR
+ Most Rev. Howard J. Hubbard
Bishop of Albany, NY

October 4, 2000

The Nihil Obstat and Imprimatur are official declarations that a book or pamphlet is free of doctrinal or moral error.

ARTWORK
Clip art is taken from *Catholic Clip Art on CD*. Reprinted with permission of Liguori Publications, Liguori, MO 63057-9999. No other reproduction of this material is permitted.

Published by GBS, Inc.
PO Box 557
465 Saratoga Street
Cohoes, NY 12147

ISBN #- 0-9706932-0-6

Printed in the United States of America

Acknowledgements

Few things in life are accomplished without the help of others. Such is the case with this book. I want to express my deep gratitude to Steve and Jill Baboulis and Steve and Patty Lescarbeau for their support and encouragement. Their gifts of time, talent and treasure have made this book possible.

Throughout my life, I have been fortunate to have crossed paths with many fine priests, sisters and brothers. In many ways, I owe my priesthood to them. As such, all profits resulting from this book will go toward the retirement needs of priests, sisters and brothers.

I want to acknowledge Liguori Publications for the use of their *Catholic Clip Art on CD*.

Finally, I want to thank the many people who I have had the privilege to serve as a priest. They have enriched my life in so many ways. I have learned a great deal about Jesus Christ from them and their example of faith continues to motivate me each day.

Contents

CONTENTS

CONTENTS

Perseverance

At that time there shall arise Michael, the great prince; it shall be a time unsurpassed in distress since nations began until that time. At that time your people shall escape, everyone who is found written in the book. Many of those who sleep in the dust of the earth shall awake; some shall live forever, others shall be an everlasting horror and disgrace. But the wise shall shine brightly like the splendor of the firmament. And those who lead the many to justice shall be like the stars forever.

From Daniel 12

The Book of Daniel is often difficult to understand because it is written in a poetic style and is very symbolic. In a nutshell, it is a book that encourages people to persevere in difficult times.

So often in life, we are asked to carry several crosses simultaneously, and they can get very heavy. It wouldn't be as bad if we had only to carry one cross at a time, but often we are asked to carry more than one, as in the expression, "when it rains, it pours." When everything seems to be caving in around us, that's when we can begin to lose our faith and that's when the message of perseverance has something to say to us.

On this topic I am reminded of something I once read about Winston Churchill. As a young boy, his parents had little time for him. He failed miserably at school. Later, he experienced one political failure after another. However, when his country needed him the most, his greatness came through. The key to Churchill's success can be traced to a five-word commencement address he delivered at Harrow, the boarding school he attended as a youth. Churchill said, "Never, never, never give up." During times of great stress and turmoil, Jesus would give us similar advice: no matter what, never, never, never give up your faith...persevere no matter what.

1

Gifts From God

There are different gifts but the same Spirit; there are different ministries but the same Lord; there are different works but the same God who accomplishes all of them in everyone. To each person the manifestation of the Spirit is given for the common good. To one the Spirit gives his wisdom in discourse, to another the power to express knowledge. Through the Spirit one receives faith; by the same Spirit another is given the gift of healing, and still another miraculous powers. Prophecy is given to one; to another power to distinguish one spirit from another. One receives the gift of tongues, another that of interpreting the tongues. But it is one and the same Spirit who produces all these gifts, distributing them to each as he wills.

From Corinthians 12

A good friend of mine worked for a large engineering company and one of their consultants at the time was a former Kennedy administration cabinet member. My friend tells how this man could walk into a room of 400 people he had never met and work his way through the room in a couple of hours. The following year he would return and could remember everyone's name, including the names of their spouses, even though he had no contact with them during the year. Now that's a gift…a God-given gift.

St. Paul talks about gifts in the reading from Corinthians and he tells us two important things about the gifts given to us by God. First, Paul tells us that everyone has been given gifts by God and that all gifts are important. Some people get very down on themselves because they believe that they have no gifts. That's wrong because everyone has gifts. Granted, sometimes we don't have a lot of the more identifiable or public gifts. These types of gifts would include things like intelligence, athletic ability, musical or artistic talent, or the ability to recall names. But there are other,

2

maybe less noticeable gifts that are equally important. Gifts such as gentleness, patience, compassion, and love for others. God has blessed everyone with gifts, equally important gifts. Don't ever sell yourself short and don't let others sell themselves short either.

Second, St. Paul tells us that God's gifts are to be used for the good of the community...for the good of those around us. So often gifts are seen as something personal, for one's own use and benefit only. St. Paul says no, individual gifts are to be shared with others and that it is the reason God gave us these gifts. We all have a responsibility not to waste our God-given gifts because they are for the benefit of all.

On a final note, it is normal for us to wish that we had gifts which others have. But when we dwell on it, when we let it get under our skin, we get caught in the ugly web of jealousy. When others have gifts that we don't have, rejoice and be happy for them; don't be jealous of them, because, as Francis Rochefoucauld once said, jealousy contains more self-love than love.

Decisive Moments

Jesus took Peter, James, and John off by themselves with him and led them up a high mountain. He was transfigured before their eyes and his clothes became dazzling white...Elijah appeared to them along with Moses; the two were in conversation with Jesus. Then Peter spoke to Jesus, "Rabbi, how good it is for us to be here. Let us erect three booths on this site, one for you, one for Moses, and one for Elijah." He hardly knew what to say, for they were all overcome with awe. A cloud came, overshadowing them, and out of the cloud a voice: "This is my Son, my beloved. Listen to him."

From Mark 9

Do you remember an Olympic athlete by the name of Dan Jansen? In the late 1980's and early 1990's, Dan Jansen was the world's best men's speed skater. In two Olympic Games prior to the Norway Olympics, he failed to win a gold medal, even though he was the world's best. I remember that in one of those races, the untimely death of his sister caused him to lose concentration and he fell during the competition. However, in the Norway Olympics, during his last opportunity, he finally won an Olympic gold medal. I'll never forget that at the medal ceremony, toward the end of the national anthem, Dan Jansen looked up and pointed toward heaven. Later, he said that he was pointing to his late sister. When asked to describe that moment, he was unable to find the right words. Dan Jansen had experienced a transfiguration moment, a decisive moment in his life. For a fleeting moment, he experienced a world beyond *this* world.

In Mark's account, Peter, James, and John also experienced a decisive moment in their lives. It was the transfiguration of our Lord. For a few precious moments they saw Jesus in a totally different way, and this experience had an impact on their lives

4

forever. The apostles and Dan Jansen aren't the only ones who have experienced transfiguration moments in their lives. You and I have, or will, experience them. I suspect that the maternity floors of hospitals are common sites for transfiguration moments. For example, when parents hold their newborn in their arms for the first time and say, "This is a miracle." Like Dan Jansen, they are probably unable to adequately describe the experience. Other transfiguration moments might include hearing the words, "Your tumor is benign, not malignant," or, perhaps after years of hostility we hear or say the words, "I forgive you" or "I'm sorry."

Transfiguration experiences are ordinary events experienced in an extraordinary way. They are God shining through in the people and events that surround us. Hold onto your transfiguration moments. Share those little glimpses of Jesus with family and friends; they don't come along often. They are like little treasures. No, we can't deposit them in a bank, but they are worth more than anything money can buy.

Long-Term Happiness

Jesus summoned the crowd again and said to them, "Hear me, all of you, and try to understand. Nothing that enters a man from outside can make him impure; that which comes out of him, and only that, constitutes impurity. Let everyone heed what he hears!" "Wicked designs come from the deep recesses of the heart: acts of fornication, theft, murder, adulterous conduct, greed, maliciousness, deceit, sensuality, envy, blasphemy, arrogance, and obtuse spirit. All these evils come from within and render a man impure."

From Mark 7

There are all kinds of polls: NBC news polls, Gallup polls, and the CNN/USA Today poll, to name a few. I take a big interest in polls because I think they tell a great deal about human nature at a particular point and time in history. I would love to see the results of a poll that asks this question: As an individual, what do you want most from life? It's hard to predict, but I'd guess that if that question were asked in a poll, the most frequent answer would be happiness. I think that's what people want most out of life... happiness.

Here's a thought for your consideration. Following God's laws is a simple formula for happiness. Most of the time we see God's laws as limiting us, as restrictions on our personal freedom. Yet, the commandments, the beatitudes, and all of Jesus' teachings are really a simple formula for long-term happiness. Will living out Jesus' teachings involve occasional self-denial and sacrifice? Absolutely. The choice not to follow God's laws may bring short-term happiness but it won't bring long-term happiness. All we have to do is look at our society to see what happens when God's laws are ignored. What are some of the poisons of life-long happiness? Jesus talks about some of them in the above reading: acts of fornication, theft, murder, adultery, greed, malice, deceit, envy, blasphemy, arrogance and an obtuse spirit…all of these are killers of long-term happiness and all violate God's laws.

If we desire long-term happiness in our lives we haven't got to go to the bookstore for the latest psychological insights into the human brain. The answers are in the scriptures.

Struggling With Faith

On the evening of that first day of the week, even though the disciples had locked the doors of the place where they were ... Jesus came and stood before them. "Peace be with you," he said. At the sign of the Lord the disciples rejoiced. It happened that one of the Twelve, Thomas, was absent when Jesus came. A week later the disciples were once more in the room, and this time Thomas was with them. Despite the locked doors, Jesus came and stood before them. "Peace be with you," he said; then, to Thomas: "Take your finger and examine my hands. Put your hand into my side. Do not persist in your unbelief, but believe!" Thomas said in response, "My Lord and my God!" Jesus then said to him: "You became a believer because you saw me. Blest are they who have not seen and have believed."

From John 20

On occasion people approach me and almost ashamedly say, "I'm struggling with my belief in God." Sometimes that struggle is because of a personal tragedy. Maybe it comes about as a result of coming face to face with science...the realization that science can always be more tangible than faith because faith cannot be proven. At other times, the struggle is a result of reflection on pain throughout the world and of our asking ourselves, "How could an all knowing, powerful and loving God allow this?"

I always tell people struggling with their faith not to be ashamed. Struggle with belief is something people young and old, male and female all face at times. It's part of being human. Struggle with belief happened to one of Jesus' chosen twelve; it happened to Thomas.

For Thomas, belief was based on the ability to see and touch our Lord. We're no different; we'd love for Jesus to come and sit in our living rooms where we could touch him and talk to him. But then, that wouldn't be faith anymore; it would be proof. Faith always involves a blind leap. Faith is something we practice without total proof.

Our Lord understands how difficult it is to believe in someone we have never touched or seen, and I think someday when we meet Jesus in heaven, we're going to find out that he is more proud of us than we've given ourselves credit for. I base that thought on the comment made to Thomas by our Lord: "Thomas you became a believer because you saw me. Blest are they who have not seen and have believed."

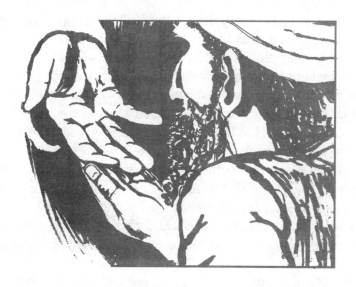

Making Decisions

In you, O Lord, I take refuge;
*   Let me never be put to shame.*
In your justice rescue me,
*   incline your ear to me,*
*   make haste to deliver me!*
Be my rock of refuge,
*   a stronghold to give me safety.*
You are my rock and my fortress;
*   for your name's sake you will lead and guide me.*

From Psalm 31

Throughout our lives, we come to many crossroads, crossroads that require major decisions. For example, one might ponder questions such as these: Which school or college should I attend and in what field should I use my gifts and talents? Is this the person whom I should marry? Should I change jobs or should I take the promotion that will require us to move? Should I have the surgery or not? Should we sell our home because we are no longer able to care for it? Hundreds of major decisions face all of us in the course of our lifetimes.

When we come to the crossroads of life, we do a pretty good job of analyzing all the pluses and minuses of our options. But do we ask God where he might be leading us? Do we consult God as to which direction we should choose at the crossroads? The psalmist suggests we do because God will lead us and guide us.

A retired couple once came to me and told me about their decision to sell their home of many years and to relocate to a warmer climate. They told me, "We really feel our Lord calling us to make this change in our lives. We have prayed about this decision for months and we feel very comfortable with our decision." I was very impressed with the process that they went through in making their decision. I was impressed because the first thing they did was involve our Lord in the decision-making process; they made God a major player. Sometimes we forget to consult our Lord. Secondly, they realized that answers from God don't come overnight. We need to listen to our hearts over a period of weeks or months, maybe years. Third, they took the time to listen to God on a frequent basis. Unless we listen, we will never hear God in our hearts. Fourth, once they made their decision, they checked their hearts and found that they were content and at peace. That's the litmus test for our decisions: Is there peace and contentment?

The bottom line is this: God desperately wants to be involved in our lives, especially when we are trying to make major decisions, but we must first ask for his guidance. When we come to the crossroads of life, let us consult our Lord and be open to where he is leading us.

The Light of Christ

Jesus said to his disciples: "You are the light of the world. A city set on a mountain cannot be hidden. Nor do they light a lamp and then put it under a bushel basket; it is set on a lampstand where it gives light to all in the house. Just so, your light must shine before others."

From Matthew 5

I always consider it a great privilege to celebrate a funeral. I'll never forget a funeral I celebrated for an elderly woman about a year ago. The deceased was a woman who had never married and had no living relatives. Further, she had outlived all of her friends. As I walked down the aisle of the church at the beginning of the funeral liturgy, there was no one in the pews. When I arrived at the casket, there were two young women standing behind it. For the next hour, the three of us celebrated the life of the deceased woman. At the cemetery, I was surprised to again see the two young women. After the committal prayers, I inquired as to how they knew the deceased. One woman told me that she was the legal guardian of the deceased. The other woman, a Roman Catholic, told me that she was a friend of the legal guardian and, because the legal guardian was Jewish and unsure of what to do at a Catholic funeral liturgy, she had decided to accompany her friend to the funeral. She went on to say that she had not planned on coming to the cemetery but, because the deceased had no family or friends, she wanted to come to the cemetery to pray for her. She related, "I thought it was important that someone be here for this woman."

The actions of that young woman really touched my heart. She had taken time off to come to the funeral in support of her friend and then felt a need to pray at the cemetery for someone she had never met. When I read the gospel passage where Jesus speaks

12

of being a light that shines before others, I thought of that young woman. Her example was a powerful light and, for me, her actions reflected the compassion, love and selflessness of Jesus Christ. She was a light in such a humble way; there were no cameras or newspaper reporters or anyone to thank her for her efforts. She simply went about the work of Christ in a quiet, unassuming manner.

We are all called to be the light of Christ for others. As someone once said, "Preach the gospel; use words if necessary."

The First Question

Jesus said to his disciples: "When the Son of Man comes in his glory, escorted by all the angels of heaven, he will sit upon his royal throne, and all the nations will be assembled before him. Then he will separate them into two groups, as a shepherd separates sheep from goats. The sheep he will place on his right hand, the goats on his left. The king will say to those on his right: 'Come. You have my Father's blessing! Inherit the kingdom prepared for you from the creation of the world. For I was hungry and you gave me food, I was thirsty and you gave me drink. I was a stranger and you welcomed me, naked, and you clothed me. I was ill and you comforted me in prison and you came to visit me.' Then the just will ask him: "Lord, when did we see you hungry and feed you or see you thirsty and give you drink? When did we welcome you away from home or clothe you in your nakedness? When did we visit you when you were ill or in prison?' The king will answer them: "I assure you, as often as you did it for one of my least brothers or sisters, you did it for me.'

From Matthew 25

When we die, and judgment day comes, what do you think will be the first question our Lord will ask us? Do you think he will ask us if we ever became the president of a company of if we became a successful business person? Do you think he will ask us about the house we lived in, the car we drove or the clothes we wore? Do you think he will ask me how many babies I baptized, marriages I witnessed or confessions I heard? No, I don't think Jesus will ask those questions.

The first question I think Jesus is going to ask all of us is: "Did you love me and did you love my people?" I base this guess on the frequency with which Jesus speaks to those topics in scripture. Matthew's gospel is but one example of this.

14

Loving God's little people...those who are hungry, strangers, naked, ill or imprisoned...can become a burdensome, thankless and frustrating experience over a period of time. But if we see the face of Jesus Christ in the marginalized people who cross our path, loving them becomes a privilege and not a burden. Why? Because it was Jesus who said: "As often as you did it for one of my least brothers or sisters, you did it for me."

Staying Focused

The angel Gabriel was sent from God to a town of Galilee named Nazareth, to a virgin betrothed to a man named Joseph, of the house of David. The virgin's name was Mary. Upon arriving, the angel said to her, "Rejoice, O highly favored daughter! The Lord is with you. Blessed are you among women..." The angel went on to say to her, "Do not fear, Mary. You have found favor with God. You shall conceive and bear a son and give him the name Jesus"...Mary said to the angel, "How can this be since I do not know man?" The angel said to her, "The Holy Spirit will come upon you and the power of the Most High will overshadow you; hence, the holy offspring to be born will be called Son of God."

From Luke 1

During the holidays, we hear a lot of talk about the dangers of drinking and driving. Ads on the radio, television, and in the newspapers tell us that alcohol and cars are a potentially dangerous combination, and for good reason. There is another potentially deadly combination, one that we don't hear much about; it's called being overwhelmed with life, combined with a lack of hope.

Some years ago, the newspapers carried a story about Jeff Alm. Jeff Alm was a twenty-five year old professional football player for the then-Houston Oilers. He was a Notre Dame graduate and a former All-American at the school. At a young age, Jeff took his own life. He had become overwhelmed with the problems of living and had lost any sense of hope.

Reflecting on the reading above, we might imagine that Mary felt overwhelmed when the angel Gabriel asked if she would carry the Son of God in her womb. She must have had a sense of being overwhelmed most of her life; can you imagine being the one

16

who would teach Jesus how to love, forgive, and respect others? Though Mary must have felt overwhelmed, she always kept alive the flame of hope in her heart. She knew she was doing God's will and she never let her problems or struggles blur her focus on the light at the end of the tunnel. That light is eternal life with God in heaven.

We can all relate to being overwhelmed at times. Pressures from school, a job, our family or society can all contribute to that feeling. Although we try to avoid being overwhelmed, it's a part of life. It happens to all of us sooner or later. Although we may feel overwhelmed at times, we must keep focused on the light at the end of the tunnel. That's one of the reasons we come to Church every week...to keep hope alive and to celebrate hope.

Two thousand years ago a baby was born in Bethlehem, a baby who was to change the world forever. One of the things this baby brought, and continues to bring, is hope. Stay focused, never lose hope, no matter how overwhelming things may seem at times.

Choosing Life

I will never forget you. See, upon the palms of my hands I have written your name.

From Isaiah 49

A couple of years ago, I spent about two weeks in the Holy Land. One day while our group was touring in Jerusalem, we decided that we would visit the holocaust museum (Yad Veshem). Part of the museum is a section devoted to the 1.5 million babies and young children who were killed as part of the holocaust. The architect of the children's museum had a unique way of getting his point across. As you walked into the museum, there was no lighting, only thousands of tiny light bulbs all around you; these represented the lives lost during the holocaust. Through the use of mirrors, the architect was able to portray the vastness of 1.5 million babies and children. As you proceeded through the darkened hallways, names were read of some of the babies who were killed during the holocaust. Yet, the architect went one step further. Toward the end of the darkened museum, after a visitor would have had sufficient time to digest the immensity of the 1.5 million lights and hearing many of the names read, the architect hung pictures of some of the babies who had been killed, not allowing the museum visitors to insulate themselves by opting for the concept of "out of sight, out of mind." No, the architect made you put a face to a name, and that's when I lost it. When you put a face on something, it's a whole new ball game.

Remember the news story about Susan Smith? She was the young mother from South Carolina who arranged to have her two young children drowned while strapped into a car several years ago. We all saw the pictures of the two beautiful children on television and in the paper, and we fell in love with them. This country was outraged over her actions. Yet, if she had decided to abort those two children months before their births, not a peep would have been heard. Why? Because there wouldn't have been any faces to fall in love with, it would have been "out of sight, out of mind."

If we were to design a museum honoring the babies killed by abortion in this country since 1973, we would need more than thirty million little lights, and if we were able to draw pictures of what those babies' faces might have looked like, say through computer imaging or enhancement, none of us would be able to make it through that museum without being overcome with grief. If we were able to put faces on those thirty million babies, this country would demand an immediate end to abortion.

Today, more than ever, is a time to pray for the victims of abortion, both the dead and the living, and maybe most important, it's a time to reflect on the tragedy that results when human beings decide to play God…when human beings take it upon themselves to determine who lives and who dies.

Love One Another

Jesus said to his disciples, "As the Father has loved me, so I have loved you. Live on in my love. You will live in my love if you keep my commandments, even as I have kept my Father's commandments, and live in his love. All this I tell you that my joy may be yours and your joy may be complete. This is my commandment: love one another as I have loved you. There is no greater love than this: to lay down one's life for one's friends."

From John 15

I recall an unusual happening in Albany, New York, some years ago. A seal had made its way up the Hudson River to the Port of Albany and spent several days there. Many people took great interest in the seal. Several weeks later it was reported that the seal had died somewhere down toward New York City. The story made headlines; it was on the front page of the newspaper, and it was the lead story on the television news. The death of a seal was the top story. At that time, I can remember thinking to myself that there are forty thousand people in Africa who will starve to death today and there will be little or no mention of them in the newspapers or on television. Why? Because tragedies such as starving people in the world are old news. Experts would say that news of that sort no longer interests people.

It worries me that increasingly, we are getting away from the message of John's scriptural passage. That message is, "love one another." When Jesus said to "love one another" he was referring to human beings because only humans are made in the image and likeness of God. The commandment, "love one another" doesn't refer to seals, cars, dollars, hobbies, jobs, houses, land, fame, or power…it refers to human beings. When people aren't the primary focus of our love, atrocities occur. It's been that way throughout all of history, right up to the present. Revel Howe once said something similar to the following: God created people to be loved and things to be used. When the order is reversed, so that things are loved and people are used, tragedy results...tragedy results.

Reconciliation

Put on then, as God's chosen ones, holy and beloved, heart-felt compassion, kindness, humility, gentleness, and patience, bearing with one another and forgiving one another, if one has a grievance against another, as the Lord has forgiven you, so must you also do.

From Colossians 3

In light of a decision made by our country a few years ago to normalize relations with Vietnam, many American companies are attempting to do business in that country. A friend of mine is a mining engineer whose company was trying to win a contract with the Vietnamese government to develop a coal mine around Hanoi. Recently, my buddy was telling me a story about a dinner that he and two co-workers had one evening in Hanoi with representatives from the Vietnamese government. Before the meal began, one of the Vietnamese government officials identified himself as a former North Vietnamese Army officer. He then went on to ask if any of the three Americans seated at the table had fought in Vietnam. One of my friend's co-workers acknowledged that he had. My buddy said that at that moment there was a real feeling of tension and uncertainty in the air. Then, the former North Vietnamese Army officer picked up a tin cup filled with some of the locally grown wine, looked at the former American soldier, proposed a toast and said, "To old enemies and to new friends." My friend said that at the moment the two former enemies toasted one another, he felt chills go up and down his spine because there was a real feeling of reconciliation in the room.

We are asked to forgive those who have hurt us in the same measure that God has forgiven us. Forgiving those who have hurt us is one of the hardest things that God asks us to do in this life.

However, when long awaited forgiveness is given, or received, it is enough to send chills up and down our spines.

When Faith is Shaken

[After the disciples heard Jesus proclaim that he is "the bread from heaven," they remarked,] "This sort of talk is hard to endure. How can anyone take it seriously?" Jesus was fully aware that his disciples were murmuring in protest at what he had said. "Does it shake your faith?" he asked them. "What, then, if you were to see the Son of Man ascend to where he was before? It is the spirit that gives life; the flesh is useless. The words I spoke to you are spirit and life. Yet among you there are some who do not believe ... This is why I have told you that no one can come to me unless it is granted him by the Father." From this time on, many of the disciples broke away and would not remain in his company any longer. Jesus then said to the Twelve, "Do you want to leave me too?" Simon Peter answered him, "Lord, to whom shall we go? You have the words of eternal life."

From John 6

Jesus asks: "Does it shake your faith?" Does it shake your faith when you watch on television hundreds of thousands of Africans suffering and dying from war, famine and disease? Does it shake your faith when tragedy strikes you, a member of your family or someone in your circle of friends? Does it shake your faith when your prayers seemingly go unanswered or are answered in a way you didn't want? Speaking for myself, it shakes my faith...right to its very core.

Two thousand years ago, the disciples' faith was shaken because they couldn't totally understand the ways of our Lord; they found some of what he said difficult to believe and endure. Struggling with our faith is part of being human. It happened to the disciples two thousand years ago and it happens to us today. The question arises, "What do we do when our faith is shaken? How do we react?" Well, we have the same two options that the followers of Christ had in the above reading:

24

Option 1 -- Leave the faith. Some of Jesus' followers decided that what Jesus was saying didn't match their human experience or human knowledge, therefore, it couldn't be correct and so they left him.

Option 2 -- This was the option taken by the disciples. They decided to hang in there despite not being able to totally understand the ways of our Lord. They decided to continue to follow him, to continue to have faith in him. Why did they do that? Peter answered that question best when he said, "Lord, to whom shall we go? You have the words of eternal life." That's the same reason we continue to follow our Lord, even when our faith has been shaken...shaken to its very core.

The Commandments

*God delivered all these commandments: "I, the Lord, am
your God, who brought you out of the land of Egypt, that place of
slavery. You shall not have other gods besides me... You shall not
take the name of the Lord, your God, in vain... Remember to keep
holy the Sabbath day... Honor your father and your mother, that
you may have a long life in the land which the Lord, your God, is
giving you. You shall not kill. You shall not commit adultery. You
shall not steal. You shall not bear false witness against your
neighbor. You shall not covet your neighbor's house. You shall
not covet your neighbor's wife... nor anything else that belongs to
him.*

From Exodus 20

Topographic maps are a must for any hiker. They are
especially useful in hiking because they help one determine the
best route to gain access to the top of the mountain. I recall one
day a buddy and I were climbing a mountain near Buena Vista,
Colorado; its peak was about 14,000 feet above sea level. We had
studied the topographic maps and had determined the best route to
the top. About a third of the way up to the peak, we thought we
saw a shortcut to the top; at least that's how it appeared from our
vantage point. So we pursued the shortcut only to find that we had
come to a dead end. We could go no further. We had come to a
rock face that we could not climb, so we had to backtrack and
resume our original plan. Making a decision based on a limited
perspective had gotten us into trouble. We'd forgotten that maps
don't lie. If you want to get to the top of the mountain, you've got
to follow the map.

Like the topographical map, the Ten Commandments keep
us on the right trail in life. When we don't follow them, we come
to a dead end. The commandments are very basic. They urge us to

keep God as the priority in our lives, use God's name only with the greatest respect, attend Mass on Sundays, love and respect members of our family, protect the sanctity of all human life, use the gift of human sexuality as intended by God, act honestly and fairly, tell the truth, and keep tabs on our thoughts and desires.

The Ten Commandments are like a topographic map, because if we follow them, they will lead us straight to the peak...heaven.

Heaven

For God so loved the world that he gave his only son, so that everyone who believes in him might not perish but might have eternal life. For God did not send his son into the world to condemn the world, but that the world might be saved through him.

If a non-Christian asked you, "Please summarize for me in one sentence what the Christian faith is all about," how would you answer that question? Any of us would be hard-pressed to come up with anything better than John, chapter 3, verse 16 which reads: "For God so loved the world that he gave his only son so that everyone who believes in him might not perish but might have eternal life." They are some of the most memorable words in all of scripture.

Note that the last words of John 3:16 promise us eternal life. Someone once said to me, "You're always talking about heaven and eternal life, but I am very happy here in this life. Can you tell me why I should look forward to going to heaven?" That's a fair question and a good one. Let me address that by referring to Plato's Republic. One section of that work is called "The Myth of the Cave." The setting is an underground cave and the story involves five or six people who have been in the cave since infancy. Their necks, hands and legs are chained. They have stayed in the same place all their lives. The only light is provided by a fire which burns behind them. Therefore, the only things they experience are the shadows that the fire casts on the walls of the cave in front of them. Then, one day, an inhabitant of the cave is led outside. For the first time he experiences the sun, sky, grass, mountains, wild creatures, wind, etc. Once outside the cave, that individual was exposed to a world he never knew existed. It was beyond what he

28

ever had experienced.

Our life on earth is like the lives of those in the cave; it is a limited experience. We are happy with it because we've never experienced anything different. By staying faithful to God, we are promised that we will be led out of the cave of earthly life, to a beautiful life in heaven that we have yet to know. That event will be the greatest moment we have ever experienced.

The Proper Perspective

In Isaiah the prophet it is written: "I send my messenger before you to prepare your way: a herald's voice in the desert crying, 'Make ready the way of the Lord, clear him a straight path.'"

Thus it was that John the Baptizer appeared in the desert proclaiming a baptism of repentance that led to forgiveness of sins. All the Judean countryside and the people of Jerusalem went out to him in great numbers. They were being baptized by him in the Jordan River as they confessed their sins ... The theme of his preaching was: "One more powerful than I is to come after me. I am not fit to stoop and untie his sandal straps. I have baptized you in water: He will baptize you in the Holy Spirit."

From Mark 1

John the Baptizer must have had his hands full. His assignment was to get a large number of people prepared for the coming of Jesus. That must have been a difficult job because the people in Jesus' time were very busy people; they had to work hard just to survive. Like us, they probably had very little free time, but John the Baptizer's assignment was to get the people to step back and put things in perspective. He was trying to get the people to see that the ordinary details of life were insignificant compared to the coming of Jesus Christ.

Perhaps you have come across the following letter at some time in the past. It speaks to the issue of having the proper perspective:

Dear Mom and Dad:

I'm sorry to be so long in writing again, but all my writing paper was lost the night the dormitory was burned down by the demonstrators. I'm out of the

30

hospital now, and the doctor says my eyesight should be back to normal sooner or later.   I received quite a large bill from the hospital and I told them to send it to you. The wonderful boy, Bill, who rescued me from the fire kindly offered to share his little apartment with me until the dorm is rebuilt next year.   He comes from a good family, so you won't be too surprised when I tell you we are going to get married.   In fact, you always wanted a grandchild so you will be glad to know that you will be grandparents next month.

Your loving daughter,

Mary

P.S.   Please disregard the above.   There was no fire, I haven't been in the hospital, I'm not pregnant, and I don't even have a boyfriend. But I did get a "D" in French and an "F" in chemistry, and I wanted to be sure you received this news with the proper perspective.

Love,

Mary

The season of Advent calls us to put the birth of Jesus in its proper perspective. Christmas isn't really about tinsel or cookies or presents or Christmas trees or parties…it's about Jesus Christ…the love, the hope and the peace of Jesus Christ. Everything else is details, simply details.

Pain and Suffering

"Come to me, all you who are weary and find life burdensome and I will refresh you. Take my yoke upon your shoulders and learn from me, for I am gentle and humble of heart. Your souls will find rest, for my yoke is easy and my burden light."

From Matthew 11

On Sunday afternoon, I always look over the scripture readings for the following Sunday. That way I have a full week to reflect on the next Sunday's scriptures. Inevitably, I will come across something during the week that becomes the basis of my Sunday homily. This past week, I thought of two very sad events. First, many of our young people had heavy hearts this week upon learning of the tragic death of their friend, Lindsey Baron. Second, it was one week ago this evening that the memorial service was held in Florida for nineteen Air Force personnel killed in the terrorist bomb blast in Saudi Arabia. I thought of our young people and those families in Florida when I read the gospel passage above, where Jesus says, "Come to me, all you who are weary and find life burdensome and I will refresh you."

There are no adequate human answers to the questions of pain and suffering. We will find peace in our lives only when we turn it all over to God: our frustration, our anxieties, our anger and our pain. Peace in our lives will come only when we say, "God, I don't understand all of your ways, but I'm going to trust that you know what you're doing…that you're steering this ship and you know where it's going. Lord, I'm going to trust that someday in heaven you'll explain to me why bad things happen to good people, that you'll show me how pain and suffering fit into your overall plan of salvation." Only when we turn over to God all our unanswered questions, pain, frustrations and sufferings, will we ever have peace in our lives, real peace of mind and heart. That's why Jesus said, "Come to me, all you who are weary and find life burdensome and I will refresh you."

Meeting Society's Expectations

Thus says the Lord...I have called you by name: you are mine. When you pass through the water, I will be with you; in the rivers you shall not drown. When you walk through fire, you shall not be burned; the flames shall not consume you. For I am the Lord, your God...you are precious in my eyes.

From Isaiah 43

God said, "I have called you by name: you are mine...you are precious in my eyes." Do you believe that? Do you really? A lot of people don't. They may have heard it, but they've never soaked it up, never internalized it. Recently, the paper carried a story about a fourteen-year-old boy who took his own life the day before the start of school. He was overweight and feared that people would make fun of him. Somewhere along the line he got the impression that if you're not slim and trim, if you're not perfect, there is no room for you in this society. Isn't that sad; he never absorbed the words, "I have called you by name: you are mine...you are precious in my eyes."

In our highly driven society, one wonders if there is room for second best. What happens to the one who is not the prettiest, the smartest, the wittiest, the most successful, the best athlete or the most popular? How about the person who comes in last place? We spend a lot of energy trying to meet society's expectations don't we? But God doesn't care about society's expectations. He doesn't care about the clothes we wear, the car we drive, the house we live in, the job we have, our educational degrees or our physical appearance...he doesn't care. God made us the way we are because he liked it very much.

When we feel that we don't "measure up", when we have been called a "loser" or a "failure", perhaps we should spend some time with the beautiful words of Isaiah 43. They speak of God's great love for us as individuals and his certainty in creating us.

May I suggest not simply reading the words from Isaiah 43. Rather, take the time to absorb the words. When we really absorb and believe those words, society's expectations will seem less and less important to us.

Christian Witness

In those days Peter stood in the midst of the brothers..."Brothers," he said, "the saying in Scripture uttered long ago by the Holy Spirit through the mouth of David was destined to be fulfilled in Judas, the one who guided those who arrested Jesus. He was one of our number and he had been given a share in this ministry of ours. It is written in the Book of Psalms, 'May another take his office.'"

It is entirely fitting, therefore, that one of those who was of our company while the Lord Jesus moved among us, from the Baptism of John until the day he was taken up from us, should be named as witness with us to his resurrection..." The choice fell to Matthias, who was added to the eleven apostles.

From Acts 1

After Judas Iscariot abandoned Jesus, who took his place as the twelfth apostle? If that should ever be a "Final Jeopardy" question some evening on television, you will know the answer. It was Matthias who took the place of Judas Iscariot after he betrayed our Lord. Why did Peter and the other apostles choose Matthias? We are told that their criteria for selection were for someone who had been with Jesus from his baptism through his death, resurrection, and ascension. However, there must have been many people who fit into that category, so why Matthias? Unfortunately, we don't know much about Matthias. He is mentioned only once in the scriptures, in the Acts of the Apostles. Since Matthias was only mentioned once, he must have been a "behind-the-scenes" type of person, probably someone who let his actions do the talking. He must have been greatly respected by those around him, respected for his commitment to our Lord and for being rock solid in his faith. He must have been, in other words, a great witness to the faith in good times and in bad. For the apostles, he was probably someone who reminded them a little bit of Jesus himself.

God has blessed all of us with having a Matthias in our lives, those people who have been a tremendous influence on us and on our faith commitment. Perhaps our Matthias is, or was, a parent, grandparent, spouse, child, friend, co-worker, Mother Teresa or whomever. The Matthias in our lives is or was rock solid in their faith, sure and steady in their commitment to our Lord and a beautiful witness to the faith we profess.

Let us thank our Lord for putting the Matthias' in our lives, those special people who give us a little glimpse of Jesus. Also, Lord, please help us to remember that there are other people looking for us to be the Matthias in their lives.

Trusting God

When you come to serve the Lord, prepare yourself for trials. Be sincere of heart and steadfast, undisturbed in time of adversity. Cling to him, forsake him not; thus will your future be great. Accept whatever befalls you, in crushing misfortune be patient; for in fire gold is tested, and worthy men in the crucible of humiliation. Trust God and he will help you; make straight your ways and hope in him. You who fear the Lord, wait for his mercy, turn not away lest you fall. You who fear the Lord trust him, and your reward will not be lost.

From Sirach 2

Each fall, when I used to live in Denver, a group of buddies and I would go camping in western Nebraska. Over the years we had become quite friendly with a certain Nebraska farmer and his family. One night, over dinner, the family was telling us how every autumn they catch rattlesnakes to sell for producing anti-venom. We asked the family if they would show us the captured rattlesnakes. They led us out to an old barn that didn't have any lights and then led us to a big 55 gallon drum. Using a flashlight, the father showed us the 25 to 30 rattlesnakes in the bottom of the drum. Becoming scared, the snakes started to rattle and that sent chills up our spines. Now keep in mind that this shed we were in was pitch black and the father was the only one who had a flashlight. As we were peering down at the snakes the father declared with a straight face, "I think there are four or five snakes missing." At that moment, a sense of fear set in on us. We all wanted his flashlight to check around our feet to make sure it really *was* a cat that was rubbing against our legs. We thought the father was kidding about the missing snakes but, with his poker face, we weren't sure. Ultimately, we had to believe that he would not expose us to danger; we had to trust and have faith in him.

In our lives, we sometimes find ourselves in the midst of darkness. Perhaps we are confused by events in our lives and in the world; we are unsure what the future holds for us or not as confident in our faith as we once were. During those times of darkness we want our own flashlight to illuminate our situation. However, if we lift up our heads and listen, we will see Christ holding a flashlight in the distance saying, "Why didn't you trust I would care for you?"

The Simple Beauty of Christmas

In those days Caesar Augustus published a decree ordering a census of the whole world. Everyone was to register, each to his own town. And so Joseph went from the town of Nazareth in Galilee to Judea, to David's town of Bethlehem - because he was of the house and lineage of David - to register with Mary, his espoused wife, who was with child.

While they were there the days of her confinement were completed. She gave birth to her first-born son and wrapped him in swaddling clothes and laid him in a manger, because there was no room for them in the place where travelers lodged.

There were shepherds in the locality, living in the fields and keeping night watch by turns over their flock. The angel of the Lord appeared to them, ... and they were very much afraid. The angel said to them: "You have nothing to fear! I come to proclaim good news to you - tidings of great joy to be shared by the whole people. This day in David's city a savior has been born to you, the Messiah and Lord.

From Luke 2

I love the simplicity of it all ... I love the simplicity with which the savior of human kind was born into this world some two thousand years ago tonight.

You might expect that the birth of the savior of the world would have taken place in the finest palace. But no, it wasn't even in a room with a bed; our savior's birth took place in a barn, a mere stable with animals. You might also expect that the baby would have been wrapped in the finest clothing, perhaps silk or some other costly material. But no, Jesus' clothes were merely functional. You might expect that his parents would be from royal bloodlines; Mary and Joseph were just average people. Some might expect that the Christ child would have been placed in a crib embellished with gold. But no, little Jesus was placed in a manger, the place where cattle were fed. You'd think that great dignitaries would be the first to hear about the birth of our savior. However, the angel first announced the good news to the shepherds, the poorest and most ignorant of that time. It was all so simple.

Someone once said that there is beauty in simplicity and there is no better example of that than the birth of Jesus Christ. In reflecting on the simplicity of the Nativity, I am once again reminded of the idea that some of the most beautiful and meaningful moments in our lives center on the simple things... things like being here at Mass tonight with family and friends sharing a spiritual element that is deep within all of us. I think of things like receiving a phone call or Christmas card from an old friend after a long period of time or experiencing the beauty of a smile on the face of a baby...simple things like sharing a meal with friends, a brother you don't see often, maybe an aging father or grandmother. These and hundreds of other simple moments are the real treasures of life, aren't they? Jesus is in our midst during those simple pleasures and he highlights the beauty of those moments for us.

We live in a complex world, a world that is capable of distracting us, of consuming us, of denying us the beauty of the simple pleasures of life that God offers us. Let us not go through life so consumed with work and the details of life that we fail to see the beauty in the midst of simplicity.

41

Words

When a sieve is shaken, the husks appear; so do a man's faults when he speaks. As the test of what the potter molds is the furnace, so in his conversation is the test of a man. The fruit of a tree shows the care it has had; so too does a man's speech disclose the vent of his mind. Praise no man before he speaks, for it is then that men are tested.

From Sirach 27

Recently, I had to go to the dentist to have a root canal. Even though the dentist couldn't see inside my tooth, it was the X-ray that indicated to him that a root canal needed to be performed. What shows on the X-ray reflects what's inside the tooth. Likewise, the words that come from our mouths reflect what is in our hearts and souls. We can't see what's inside the heart or the soul. However, just as the X-ray reveals the condition of the tooth, our words indicate the condition of our hearts. That's the message from Sirach, plain and simple.

Ash Wednesday is the beginning of the holy season of Lent. Perhaps Lent is a good time to ask ourselves, "What kind of words come from my mouth? Do my words often acknowledge the virtues of others or do they note their faults? Are my words gentle or bitter, loving or hostile, complimentary or critical, life-giving or life-draining?"

Lent is a wonderful time to beautify the heart and soul... and carefully choosing our words is a good place to start.

Past Mistakes

Jesus said: "What woman, if she has ten silver pieces and loses one, does not light a lamp and sweep the house in a diligent search until she has retrieved what she lost? And when she finds it, she calls in her friends and neighbors to say, 'Rejoice with me! I have found the silver piece I lost.' I tell you, there will be the same kind of joy before the angels of God over one repentant sinner."

From Luke 15

The parable of the lost coin, like the parable of the prodigal son, speaks to the mercy and forgiveness of God. Reflecting upon these parables, I am reminded of a story I was once told about a seminarian. Shortly after entering the seminary, the man decided it was time to go to confession to reconcile with God a mistake that he had carried around with him for years. He went to reconciliation and received penance and absolution. Two weeks later he returned to the same priest and confessed again the mistake he had made years ago. The priest said to him, "I think you ought to leave the seminary." Astounded, the seminarian replied, "But why?" The priest said, "Because you don't really believe in the mercy and forgiveness of God, and if you don't believe in the mercy and forgiveness of God, how will you ever be able to teach your people about the mercy and forgiveness of God?"

It's really true; no past mistake is too big to forgive for this God of ours. We only need to believe it.

Meeting Jesus

Two disciples of Jesus that same day (the first day of the Sabbath) were making their way to a village called Emmaus...discussing as they went all that happened...Jesus approached and began to walk with them; however, they were restrained from recognizing him...Beginning then, with Moses and all the prophets, he interpreted every passage of Scripture which referred to him...

When he had seated himself with them to eat, he took bread, pronounced the blessing, then broke the bread and began to distribute it to them. With that their eyes were opened and they recognized him; whereupon he vanished from their sight. They said to one another, "Were not our hearts burning inside us as he talked to us on the road and explained the Scripture to us?" They got up immediately and returned to Jerusalem, where they found the Eleven and the rest of the company assembled. They were greeted with, "The Lord has been raised! It is true!"

From Luke, 24

I love this gospel story, the story of Jesus casually walking along the road to Emmaus with two of his disciples. I guess I love this story because it tells three great truths about Jesus' presence in our lives: first, we can experience Jesus through people we least expect; second, at the times we least expect; and third, in hindsight. I was recently reminded of this when I ran into an elderly gentleman who had what appeared to be advanced Alzheimer's disease. He was very confused, to the point where he seemed to have little idea of what was happening around him. His daughter was with him and you could see the pain in her face. Her dad was no longer what he once was, but she held him, answered his frequent questions, kissed him, hugged him and reassured him. It was impressive to watch her. However, it wasn't until that night when I was recalling the day's events that it hit me: I had met Christ through that woman. That day, through that woman, I had encountered the merciful, compassionate, loving, understanding and patient Christ. I met Christ through someone I didn't expect, at a time I didn't expect, and it was only in hindsight that I recognized Christ in her.

Jesus is alive through people in our everyday lives. Maybe it's through an unexpected compliment or thank you, maybe it's through the eyes of a baby, an offer of help, or a hug when we are hurting; maybe it's in a considerate or unselfish act.

I know that we're very busy people. But if we get a chance at night, we should look back over the day and ask ourselves, "Where did I meet Christ today?" It's amazing how frequently God reveals himself to us and, like the disciples, sometimes just thinking about it makes our hearts burn with excitement.

First Eucharist

During the meal He took bread, blessed and broke it, and gave it to [his disciples]. "Take this," He said, "This is my body." He likewise took a cup, gave thanks and passed it to them, and they all drank from it. He said to them, "This is my blood, the blood of the covenant, to be poured out on behalf of many. I solemnly assure you, I will never again drink of the fruit of the vine until the day when I drink it new in the reign of God."

From Mark 14

To our young readers who will be receiving their First Holy Communion: here is a love story about you and God. Perhaps Mom, Dad, or your religion teacher could read this story to you.

Recently, I was cleaning out my parents' attic when I found a special box, a box full of memories. My Mom had stashed away a bunch of things...art projects from school, letters I had written and some pictures of my First Communion. Those pictures made me think of you, boys and girls, because they helped me to remember that special day. I remember my teachers, where I sat in Church and I remember what the host tasted like for the very first time. I'll never forget that day; I have such wonderful memories of it! Likewise, you will never forget your First Communion.

Boys and girls, the day you receive your First Communion is all about love. It's about the love your family has for you. It's also about the love that is shared between you and God.

The love story between you and God probably began seven or eight years ago. God wanted to create someone special with unique gifts and talents, so he created you. The greatest moment of your life came when you were baptized. On that day, you were given the most important gift you will ever receive in this world: the gift of eternal life. It was given to you by God out of love. Since your baptism, God has shown his love for you many times over. For example, you've experienced God's love through your parents, grandparents, friends and teachers. As part of the love story, you, in turn, have shown your love for God in many ways. For example, when you love your Mom and Dad or a brother or sister, when it's not easy to do so, that's loving God. When you take time to say your prayers every day, that's loving God. When you're a friend to someone in school who doesn't have many friends, that's loving God. When you received the sacrament of reconciliation, that's loving God. When you go to church on Sunday, that's loving God, and when you make your First Communion, the love story between you and God will continue. A new chapter will be added to the love story.

When you receive the body and blood of our Lord, it's a gift given to you out of love by God. It's not something that God goes out and buys for you; it's a gift to you of God himself. Although God will offer this gift to you throughout your whole life, the first time will be a very special moment for you.

Thirty or forty years from now, when you're helping your Mom and Dad clean out the attic, you will come across your keepsake box. You'll open the box and probably find some pictures of your First Communion, and do you know what? Those pictures are sure to bring pure joy to your heart.

The Resurrection

When the Sabbath was over, Mary Magdalene, Mary the mother of James, and Salome brought perfumed oils with which they intended to go and anoint Jesus. Very early, just after sunrise on the first day of the week, they came to the tomb. They were saying to one another, "Who will roll back the stone for us from the entrance to the tomb?" When they looked, they found that the stone had been rolled back. (It was a huge one.) On entering the tomb they saw a young man sitting at the right, dressed in a white robe. This frightened them thoroughly, but he reassured them: "You need not be amazed! You are looking for Jesus of Nazareth, the one who was crucified. He has been raised up; he is not here. See the place where they laid him."

From Mark 16

Where were you on November 22, 1963? Many of you were not yet born; you were still just a thought of God's, but a very precious thought at that. Others of you were born at that time, but were too young to remember that day. For those who do remember, you not only remember where you were, but what you were doing when you heard that President Kennedy had been shot in Dallas. With that stunning news, this country became numb overnight. There was collective confusion and a searching for answers, because JFK had been the young "new generation" president who was to lead us through the Cold War against the Soviets, and negotiate with Castro in Cuba and Ho Chi Minh in Vietnam. Now everyone felt vulnerable; JFK's death brought about a sense of hopelessness throughout this nation.

Those who experienced that day in 1963 have a taste of what the followers of Jesus must have felt like on that first Good Friday. They had given up everything to follow Jesus. Over time he had become the center of their lives and the center of their hopes and dreams; they loved him. Then, all of a sudden, he was dead. There was shock, confusion and a searching for answers. There was *hopelessness*.

Then came that first Easter when Mary Magdalene, Mary, and Salome discovered that Jesus had risen from the dead. Hopelessness turned into joy at that moment, and the women remembered Jesus' words: I will rise again after the third day and I will come back to take you with me so that where I am you also may be.

Jesus' promise to his followers two thousand years ago applies to us today, so that we, too, will experience new life in the resurrection to come. When pain and tragedy enter our lives, when we experience periods of hopelessness, remember the resurrection...the resurrection promised to each of us by Jesus.

Humility

When Jesus came on a Sabbath to eat a meal in the house of one of the leading Pharisees, they observed him closely. He went on to address a parable to the guests, noticing how they were trying to get the places of honor at the table: "When you are invited by someone to a wedding party, do not sit in the place of honor, in case some greater dignitary has been invited. Then the host might come and say to you, 'Make room for this man,' and you would have to proceed shamefacedly to the lowest place. What you should do when you have been invited is go and sit at the lowest place, so that when your host approaches you he will say, 'My friend, come up higher.' This will win you the esteem of your fellow guests. For everyone who exalts himself shall be humbled, and he who humbles himself shall be exalted."

From Luke 14

As Catholic Christians, one of the goals in our life is to take on the characteristics of Jesus. We will never fully attain that goal because we are mere humans. Luke, chapter 14, discusses one of the characteristics that Jesus displayed during his life; the characteristic that I speak of is humility. It was Jesus who said, "Learn from me for I am meek and humble of heart."

Humility has nothing to do with putting ourselves down or denying our self-worth but it does have something to do with not having too high an opinion of ourselves. History presents this example. The physician who attended to Mao Tse Tung wrote this of the deceased Chinese leader: "Mao believed in his own legend. He never doubted that his leadership, and only his leadership, would save and transform China. Mao believed that he was the country's messiah."

It's always healthy to remember that however much we

know, we still know very little compared with the total sum of knowledge. However much we have achieved personally, we still have achieved very little in the end. However important we may believe ourselves to be, when death removes us or we retire from our job, life and work will go on just the same.

Community

The Church throughout all Judea, Galilee, and Sameria was at peace. It was being built up and walked in fear of the Lord and with the consolation of the Holy Spirit, it grew in number.

From Acts 9

One of the things that I enjoy doing with our young people is getting together with them, be it at our school or in our religious education classes, and having an open dialogue with them. I tell them that they are free to ask any questions that they would like to ask. One of their frequent questions is this: "Why do I have to go to Church? It's boring and I don't get anything out of it. Besides, I pray at home; what's the difference?" That's a good question for the students to ask and I'm pleased that they feel comfortable enough to ask me that question. I tell them five things.

First, I talk to the young people about the third commandment, which asks us to keep holy the Lord's Day. I tell them that for Christians, Sunday is the Lord's Day because that's the day Christ rose from the dead. I also level with them. I tell them that like it or not, commandments are duties and part of being a Catholic Christian is following the commandments. Second, I tell them that one of the principal ways that God speaks to us is through the readings that are proclaimed at Sunday Mass. God has something to tell each of us but we have to be there to listen. Third, I tell them that we come to Mass to receive the gift of the Eucharist, the greatest gift Jesus can give us. Before he died, Jesus could have decided to leave us bars of gold, but no, he left us something much greater...the gift of himself. Therefore, another reason we go to Church is to receive that great gift of Jesus' body and blood. Fourth, I tell them to look in the bible to see how Jesus prayed. The bible tells us that Jesus prayed by himself, but he also

52

prayed with other people and that's what we do when we come to Church on Sunday. Both private and communal prayer are important. Fifth, I tell our young people about the benefits of praying with a Church community. That's what the Acts of the Apostles is talking about…Church and community.

As we all know, life can become difficult at times, and it's not always easy to follow Jesus. It's especially difficult if you're trying to do it by yourself. But it's easier and more rewarding if you're trying to do it with other people, people who share your beliefs and who may have similar struggles. A Church community helps its members along in the journey of life. That's why many parishes have services such as food pantries and pastoral care programs…to enable parishioners to help one another. That's why we have a parish prayer book and why we pray for members who have died during the week, so that grieving members of our community know they are not alone, that they have our support and prayers.

Community. That's one of the big reasons we gather each week to worship. We are a faith community helping one another, growing with one another as we journey up the mountain to be with God in heaven.

The Cost of Discipleship

On one occasion when a great crowd was with Jesus, he turned to them and said, "If anyone comes to me without turning his back on his father and mother, his wife and his children, his brothers and sisters, indeed his very self, he cannot be my follower. Anyone who does not take up his cross and follow me cannot be my disciple. If one of you decides to build a tower, will he not first sit down and calculate the outlay to see if he has enough money to complete the project? He will do that for fear of laying the foundation and then not being able to complete the work; at which all who saw it would then jeer at him, saying, 'That man began to build what he could not finish'...In the same way, none of you can be my disciple if he does not renounce all his possessions."

From Luke 14

Direct and to the point...that's how Jesus sounds in the gospel passage above. He is outlining very clearly and very concisely the cost of discipleship. When you think about it, the most meaningful accomplishments in our lives are those that come at a high cost. For example, any academic or professional accomplishment is a result of hours and hours of sacrifice and hard work. Perhaps we are very proud of our family or friends; surely we have given a lot of ourselves in order to make those relationships so meaningful. Since our faith is very meaningful to us, it shouldn't surprise us that being a disciple of Christ will come at a high cost. It will cause us inconvenience, struggle and frustration at times.

In this reading, Jesus outlines three things that he asks of his followers. First, he wants us to follow him no matter what the price. Jesus tells us that this may involve us having to turn our back on a family member or, more likely, having someone turn their back on us because we choose to follow Christ. It may involve hearing something like this from people: "Get real…everybody does it," and our having to say, "But I don't do things that way." Second, Jesus says his disciples must pick up their crosses and follow him. He asks that all his disciples join him on the cross. Not literally of course, but there are all types of crosses…physical crosses, emotional crosses and spiritual crosses…all are heavy and burdensome. As disciples we may never understand why we are asked to carry a particular cross because we will never totally understand God's way. That makes the cross even more difficult to carry. Third, Jesus asks that we renounce our material possessions. Does that mean we must sell our houses and live under a pine tree? No, but we are asked to recognize that we can become slaves to our material possessions, or the pursuit of them, and that possessions can become like idols. It is Jesus who wants to be number one in our hearts.

Jesus never promised a rose garden here on earth to those who freely choose to follow him, but he did promise us something much more important…eternal life in heaven.

The Cross

Your attitude must be Christ's: though he was in the form of God he did not deem equality with God something to be grasped at. Rather, he emptied himself and took the form of a slave, being born in the likeness of men. He was known to be of human estate, and it was thus that he humbled himself, obediently accepting even death, death on a cross!

Because of this, God highly exalted him and bestowed on him the name above every other name. So that at Jesus' name every knee must bend in the Heavens, on the Earth, and under the Earth, and every tongue proclaim to the glory of God the Father: JESUS CHRIST IS LORD!

From Philippians 2

When I contemplate the mystery of the cross, I am reminded of a church I once entered. As you walked into the rear of the church, there was a large cross with the crucified Lord on it. It was hung low to the ground so that you could touch the shins and feet of the crucified Lord. Although the corpus was white in color, the shins and feet were darkened, because over the years, thousands of people had touched that corpus as a means of gaining strength for bearing their own heavy crosses. The church itself was locked, but you could look through the glass into the body of the church. Above the altar, there was another cross. On this cross was an image of the resurrected Lord with hands outstretched.

Symbolically speaking, those two crosses represent our lives. I say that because so much of our earthly life is spent in the rear of that church with the crucified Lord. There are those times when we relate so easily to the crucified Lord because of the heavy crosses that we carry. During those times, we can only glimpse through the window to see the risen Christ. The doors are locked;

we cannot embrace the risen Lord. However, it is through our death that the doors will open and we will walk down the aisle to heaven, where we will be able to reach up and hug and kiss the risen Lord forever. That for me is the essence of the triumph of the cross.

Sin

Jesus spoke this parable addressed to those who believed in their own self-righteousness while holding everyone else in contempt: "Two men went up to the temple to pray; one was a Pharisee, the other a tax collector. The Pharisee with head unbowed prayed in this fashion: 'I give you thanks, O God, that I am not like the rest of men- grasping, crooked, adulterous- or even like this tax collector. I fast twice a week. I pay tithes on all I possess.' The other man, however, kept his distance, not even daring to raise his eyes to Heaven. All he did was beat his breast and say, 'O God, be merciful to me, a sinner.' Believe me, this man went home from the temple justified, but the other did not. For everyone who exalts himself shall be humbled while he who humbles himself shall be exalted."

From Luke 18

In 1995, America lost Mickey Mantle. I was impressed with Mantle's comments the last few weeks of his life. Not once did I hear the baseball great talk about the 565 foot homerun shot he hit at Yankee Stadium that came within inches of clearing the outer stadium wall, something no one else has ever accomplished. In those last weeks I never heard him say, "Do you remember the great catch I made to save Don Larson's perfect game in the 1956 World Series? No, what Mickey Mantle talked about in his final weeks of life were his shortcomings. He talked about not being a very good father and not being a very good husband. He talked about how poor a role model he had been for kids. I found his humility impressive. He reminded me of the tax collector in the gospel who recognized his own shortcomings; in other words, the presence of sin in his life. I suspect that Mickey's humble attitude was impressive to our Lord when they met face to face.

It takes humility before God to recognize sin in our lives.

58

When pride reigns, we become like the pharisee who was blind to his own sinfulness. A daily examination of conscience is a wonderful spiritual gem. To review the day and to ask God with an open and humble heart: "Lord, when did I not act as you would have today" or "when would you have been embarrassed to be with me today?" It is spiritually healthy to recognize sin in our lives and to do something about it. For when we no longer recognize sin in our lives, when we never take time to stand humbly before God, we have reached a spiritual dead end. When this happens, our spiritual growth will cease to occur.

Listening To False Shepherds

Jesus said, "I am the good shepherd, the good shepherd who lays down his life for the sheep. The hired hand who is no shepherd, nor owner of the sheep, catches sight of the wolf coming and runs away, leaving the sheep to be snatched and scattered by the wolf. That is because he works for pay; he has no concern for the sheep."

"I am the good shepherd. I know my sheep and my sheep know me and I know the Father; for these sheep I will give my life."

From John 10

It's amazing how sensitive our ears are. The slightest variation in the frequency of sound can help us to differentiate one human voice from another. For example, I'm always amazed when a group of young children gathers. Even with all the noise, a mother can still pick out the voice or cry of her own child. The mother's ear is attuned to the voice of her child. The gospel tells us that sheep are attuned to the voice of their shepherd in a similar way. The implication leads us to ponder this question: Are we attuned to the voice of our shepherd, Jesus Christ?

The voice of Christ has a lot of competition today. There are many voices that want our attention. The newspaper is a good source of information about whose voices people are listening to. I flipped through a recent paper and found three other voices to which many people are attuned. The first voice is the inner voice of selfishness. That's the voice that encourages us to look out solely for "good old number one." That's the voice which says to go out there and get all we can for ourselves, and if we've got to walk on people or take advantage of them in order to do it, so be it. That's the voice being listened to by many foreign leaders, whose concerns for their own self-interests have caused thousands to die.

On a more personal level, that's the voice which tells us that we have no obligation to anyone other than ourselves and our family.

A second voice that wants our attention is the voice of peer pressure. We all have a need to "fit in." If we are young, it's a voice that can lead us to drugs, sex, and violence. If we are an adult, it can lead us into the "keeping up with the Jones'" syndrome, to the point where we are never satisfied. Peer pressure is a powerful voice.

A third voice is the voice of society. That's a voice which says "everybody does it", "don't let it bother your conscience", or "there's no right and wrong; it's all relative." For example, when is the last time you saw a movie having to do with forgiveness? It doesn't happen very often. Why? Forgiveness movies don't sell; payback movies sell. The subtle voice of society is always around us.

Following the voice of a false shepherd will lead us down a path that will eventually come to a dead end. But, following the voice of Jesus will lead us straight to heaven. Whose voice have we been following lately, our Lord's or some false shepherd's?

Feeling Overwhelmed

John, in prison, heard about the works Christ performed, and sent a message through his disciples to ask him, "Are you 'He who is to come' or do we look for another?" In reply, Jesus said to them, "Go back and report to John what you hear and see: the blind recover their sight, the cripples walk, lepers are cured, the deaf hear, dead men are raised to life, and the poor have the good news preached to them."

From Matthew 11

Archbishop Harry Flynn, a priest of the Albany, NY Diocese, is presently the Archbishop of Minneapolis-St. Paul. I have great respect for this man and when I am around him, I find myself listening carefully to his insightful comments. I once heard him say, "In all my years as a Bishop, I can honestly say that I've never felt overwhelmed," and I'm thinking to myself, "How can a person who is the spiritual leader for seven-hundred-thousand Catholics never feel overwhelmed?" When I asked Archbishop Flynn that question his response was, "It is because of the hour a day I spend in prayer with our Lord; that's why I never feel overwhelmed."

Do you think that John the Baptist was overwhelmed when he had to face the difficult task of preparing the way of the Lord? To do this, he had to call people to repentance, to change their sinful ways. As a prophet, he was critical of the society in which he lived, telling the people that they were not living up to God's ways. So unpopular was John the Baptist's message that eventually he was imprisoned and executed, but it would be my guess that John the Baptist was not overwhelmed because he was rooted so deeply in God.

How about Pope John Paul II and Mother Teresa? They are examples of modern day prophets. Like John the Baptist, they are, or were, often critical of the world's ungodly ways. As a result, the Pope can become fodder for the press because his messages often make us uncomfortable. However, when you watch him and listen to him, he never seems overwhelmed. Rather, he seems contented, confident and very much at peace. I'd be willing to bet that has a lot to do with his daily prayer life...talking heart to heart with God every day.

How about us? Are we overwhelmed? Do Christmas shopping, job deadlines, family problems and stress cause us to be overwhelmed? If so, is it because we have had no time to pray to God, no time to connect with him and feel his presence, his calm, his strength? There is an old saying that goes like this: "The most important time to pray is when we don't have time to pray," and I think there is a lot of truth to that.

Mothers

Beloved, let us love one another, because love is of God; everyone who loves is begotten by God and knows God. Whoever is without love does not know God, for God is love...Beloved, if God loved us, we also must love one another. No one has ever seen God. Yet, if we love one another, God remains in us, and his love is brought to perfection in us.

From 1 John 4

There was a terrible situation in the African country of Rwanda several years ago. An estimated 100,000 people were killed in ethnic fighting over a two month period in that country. That's nearly double the number of Americans killed in Vietnam over a thirteen-year period. What pain the Rwandan people must have experienced at that time. We can't grasp the extent of their pain because we haven't walked in their shoes. We may be able to relate to their pain in a partial way, though not in its fullness.

Likewise, when God tells us that he loves us, as he does in 1 John chapter 4, we cannot grasp totally what that means. We can't grasp totally the concept of being loved unconditionally because it is something that goes beyond our experience. But God gives us a little glimpse of what his unconditional love is like through the ordinary people in our lives. One of the instruments used by God to give us a glimpse of his unconditional love is mothers. I once went to visit a three-year-old girl from the parish who was hospitalized in the pediatric ward. When I entered the room, I found both her and her mother asleep. I returned to the room some time later to find the mother and child still asleep together. The mom was probably exhausted from being with the little girl day and night. Yet, for that little girl to always have Mom with her while she was staying in a scary place, that was a little taste of God's unconditional love. The little girl did not experience God's unconditional love in its fullest, but she got a little taste of it through her mom.

We've all had little glimpses of God through our moms. Someone once said that mothers are the closest thing we have in this life to God and heaven. If that's the case, then we have a lot to look forward to in the next life.

Families

The Lord sets a father in honor over his children; a mother's authority he confirms over her sons. He who honors his father atones for sins; he stores up riches who reveres his mother. He who honors his father is gladdened by children, and when he prays he is heard. He who reveres his father will live a long life; he obeys the Lord who brings comfort to his mother.

My son, take care of your father when he is old; grieve him not as long as he lives. Even if his mind fails, be considerate with him; revile him not in the fullness of your strength. For kindness to a father will not be forgotten, it will serve as a sin offering -- it will take lasting root.

From Sirach 3

The Feast of the Holy Family is an opportunity for us to stop and reflect upon our relationships with our own families. God asks us to honor our parents and to care for them when they are old, even if their minds fail. We are told in the scriptures that kindness to our parents will never be forgotten by God.

We live in a society where the aged are not respected the way they are in some cultures. Let us never forget that we have a God-given obligation to love and honor our parents no matter what their age...no matter what their mental or physical condition.

With regard to family relationships, you've heard the expression, "Those whom we love the most are often the ones we hurt the most." It is unfortunate, but there seems to be a lot of truth to that expression. We can be tough on family members, those whom we are supposed to love the most.

The Feast of the Holy Family is a wonderful time to ask ourselves if we have unjustly hurt someone in our family and, if so, to ask their forgiveness... to tell them that we were wrong and that we are truly sorry. Perhaps it is we who need to show compassion toward a family member who has asked for our forgiveness. Either way, life is too short for us to hold onto anger and grudges. Life is far too short for that.

Do Not Be Afraid

The Lord said to Abram: "Go forth from the land of your kinsfolk and from your father's house to a land I will show you. I will make you a great nation and I will bless you; I will make your name great, so that you will be a blessing. I will bless those who bless you and curse those who curse you. All the communities of the earth shall find blessing in you."

From Genesis 12

Our community suffered a terrible loss recently. A graduate of our high school three years ago was tragically killed in a fire at the State University of New York at Geneseo. In visiting with one of our young adults who had come home for his funeral, we talked about the tragedy of it all, but also about how scary it is ...scary to realize how fragile life is and how tragedy knows no boundaries. It's true; life can be very scary.

Abraham (Abram) must have been scared. God came to him and asked him to pick up everything and to leave the land of his ancestors. At seventy-five years of age, Abraham was asked to follow God to a land he knew not. Abraham must have been *really* scared.

In Matthew's gospel account of the transfiguration, the disciples were overcome with fear when they heard the voice of the Lord speaking to them from a cloud. What did our Lord tell them? Four simple words: "Do not be afraid. " That's what God told Abraham in his fear and that's what God tells us when we are scared.

- For example, when we experience how fragile life can be, "do not be afraid."
- When we are fearful that we are not popular with our peers, "do not be afraid."
- When we fail at something no matter how hard we try, "do not be afraid."

- When we conclude that a dream will never be realized, "do not be afraid."
- When we are married, expecting our first child and something goes wrong, "do not be afraid."
- When we wonder if we will ever be happy again, "do not be afraid."
- When we become overwhelmed with life, "do not be afraid."
- When we fear losing our job, "do not be afraid."
- When loneliness seems to have engulfed us, "do not be afraid."
- When we are being rushed to the hospital because of a sudden emergency, "do not be afraid."
- When we become frustrated because we have become forgetful and we can no longer physically do what we once did, "do not be afraid."
- When we must seek assisted living because we can no longer care for ourselves, "do not be afraid."
- When it becomes clear that God is calling us home to heaven, "do not be afraid."

No matter what we will face in our lives ahead, our Lord will be with us and, therefore, we need not be afraid.

I am with you always.

Playing It Safe

Jesus said... "*There was a man going down from Jerusalem to Jericho who fell in with robbers. They stripped him, beat him, and then went off leaving him half-dead. A priest happened to be going down the same road; he saw him but continued on. Likewise there was a Levite who came the same way; he saw him and went on. But a Samaritan who was journeying along came on him and was moved to pity at the sight. He approached him and dressed his wounds...He then hoisted him on his own beast and brought him to an inn, where he cared for him.*"

From Luke 10

I have a friend who was a Navy SEAL for about ten years. Three of those years were spent in Vietnam during the conflict in Southeast Asia. He tells the story of being with another SEAL in North Vietnam on a particular mission. They were discovered by the enemy and forced to retreat to a small area where the enemy eventually surrounded the village. My friend told what it felt like to know that he was going to die. All of a sudden he noticed a Buddhist monk signaling him and his friend to come to him. With no other options available, the two men ran toward the monk who then lowered them into a well. They stayed in that well not knowing if they would come out alive. Three days later, after the enemy had left the village, the Buddhist monk returned and pulled them safely from the well.

We have all had experiences with strangers who have gone out of their way to help us out of a jam. Perhaps they were not situations where strangers have saved our lives, but where strangers have deeply touched our lives. More than likely, the injured traveler in the gospel story above never forgot the Good Samaritan who went out of his way to save his life. What about the priest and

70

the Levite? Why didn't they help the injured traveler? The priest didn't help because if the traveler had actually been dead, and the priest touched him, according to custom the priest would have been considered "unclean" for seven days. That would have been an inconvenience for the priest. Regarding the Levite, he probably didn't stop because there was a chance that he, too, might be robbed and beaten, so he decided to play it safe.

Inconvenience and playing it safe...those are two reasons that we sometimes fail to reach out to strangers in need. Inconvenience, because reaching out to others might very well cause us to be late for work or an appointment, might involve an additional expense or might result in only three hours of sleep at night instead of seven hours. Playing it safe all the time can cause us to crawl into a shell where we insulate ourselves from any potential danger or harm. Granted, there is no substitute for good common sense, but once in a while we have to take a chance on humanity. We have to take a chance that there will not be a lawsuit or some kind of danger lurking with every stranger in need of help.

We are all called to be Good Samaritans. We are called to go beyond the inconveniences and the tendency to always play it safe in response to strangers in need.

God's Will

A leper approached Jesus with a request, kneeling down as he addressed him: "If you will to do so, you can cure me." Moved with pity, Jesus stretched out his hand, touched him, and said: "I do will it. Be cured." The leprosy left him then and there, and he was cured. Jesus gave him a stern warning and sent him on his way. "Not a word to anyone now," he said, "Go off and present yourself to the priest and offer for your cure what Moses prescribed. That should be a proof for them." The man went off and began to proclaim the whole matter freely, making the story public. As a result of this, it was no longer possible for Jesus to enter a town openly. He stayed in desert places; yet people kept coming to him from all sides.

From Mark 1

We have all experienced the following scenario either directly or indirectly. A young child hears the ice cream truck coming down the street. The child says, "I want some ice cream, please." Mom has a decision to make. Several questions run through her mind. For example, how long will it be until supper? Has he or she been good and deserving of ice cream? Do I have money with me to pay for the ice cream? After processing the answers to these questions, the Mom renders a decision. If the answer is yes, joy and happiness result. If the answer is no, disappointment, perhaps even anger, is the result. In either case, the child is unaware and incapable of understanding all that went into Mom's decision of "yes" or "no".

We request things from God. We ask for recovery of health, to pass an exam, or maybe to get accepted at a college, and that's good. God has told us to ask him for what we need and want. In many ways, we are like the child and God is like the mother in the ice cream analogy. We know what we want, just like the child, but many things go into God's decision of answering "yes" or "no" to our requests. God is able to view the overall plan; we are able to see only a small portion of the plan. What may make sense for us in our limited perspective might not make sense in God's overall plan. Sometimes the answer we receive from God to our request is "yes" and our reaction is one of joy. Sometimes the answer we receive from God will be "no" and our natural reaction is one of disappointment and anger, like the child. It is then that we begin to ask why. Why did God not answer my prayer or request the way I wanted? Only when we get to heaven and see God's overall plan will it make sense to us...not until then.

In Mark's gospel, the leper had a request for Jesus. Note how the leper made his request. He said to Jesus, "If you will to do so, you can cure me." He gave Jesus the option of saying "no, it is not my will." Note that the leper did *not* say, "You can cure me, so cure me." Instead, the leper said, "If you will to do so, you can cure me," and Jesus responded, "I do will it; be cured." Perhaps the leper is an example to us all, that when we are making requests or petitions to God, we would do well to add at the end of our request or petition, "If you will to do so."

Sharing Our Resources

Jesus said to his disciples... *"Make friends for yourselves through your use of this world's goods, so that when they fail you, a lasting reception will be yours. If you can trust a man in little things, you can trust him in greater, while anyone unjust in a slight matter is also unjust in a greater. If you cannot be trusted with elusive wealth, who will trust you with lasting?" "No servant can serve two masters. Either he will hate the one and love the other or be attentive to the one and despise the other. You cannot give yourself to God and money."*

From Luke 16

When we die, there is no question in my mind that Jesus will be the very first one to meet us. Who else will be in line behind Jesus to greet us at the gates of heaven? We might imagine that our deceased family members will be there, the friends we've known over the years, our favorite saints...those we have looked up to or prayed to over the years. But beyond all those closest to our hearts, who else will be in that line? I think that the less fortunate people who we've helped through our acts of generosity and kindness, those who have passed on before us, will be in that line. They are the poor people of whom the scriptures speak, people who never were able to repay us in this world, but who will be waiting to greet us as their way of thanking us when we get to heaven. When we meet Jesus on that day, he won't have to ask us if we've shared our monetary resources with those less fortunate than ourselves, he'll just look at the length of the line of people waiting to greet us and then he'll know. Jesus will know whether we willingly shared with the poor or if we turned inward with our resources.

74

We can't take our money with us when we die, but we *can* send it ahead if we are willing to joyfully share our treasure with those less fortunate than ourselves.

Reforming Our Lives

Jesus spoke this parable: "A man had a fig tree growing in his vineyard, and he came out looking for fruit on it, but did not find any. He said to the vinedresser, `Look here! For three years now I have come in search of fruit on this fig tree and found none. Cut it down. Why should it clutter the ground?' In answer, the man said, `Sir, leave it another year while I hoe around it and manure it; then perhaps it will bear fruit. If not, I shall cut it down.'"

From Luke 13

Some time ago an article appeared in a local newspaper entitled, "'I Apologize,' Drops from the Lexicon of American Ethics." The article concluded that the concept of personal accountability is on the endangered list within this country. In other words, the article claimed that Americans have a problem with accepting responsibility. Are we good at owning up to our errors? Do we have difficulty saying things like, "I'm wrong," "It's my fault," or "I'm sorry?" According to the article, Americans are proficient at saying and believing that it is the other person's fault. When that attitude, which is prevalent in our society, creeps into our spiritual life, we're in trouble. We're in trouble because it's then that we no longer recognize sin in our lives... our consciences no longer tickle us. We become indifferent to sin. We become good at justifying our actions or the lack thereof. We become numb to sin, almost as though we'd gone to the dentist's office and received a shot of novocaine.

I'm not advocating guilt trips or dressing in sack cloth and ashes, but I am saying that unless we recognize sin in our lives and accept responsibility for it, we will never be able to carry out Jesus' call to reform, to change, to transform our lives. Recognizing sin is a necessary prerequisite for change or reform to

76

occur. Being aware of our sinfulness and having a troubled conscience on occasion are signs of a healthy spiritual life.

Repent in the name of Jesus Christ.

Martyrdom

Stephen, filled with the Holy Spirit, looked to the sky above and saw the glory of God, and Jesus standing at God's right hand. "Look!" he exclaimed, "I see an opening in the sky and the Son of Man standing at God's right hand." The onlookers were shouting aloud, holding their hands over their ears as they did so. Then they rushed at him as one man, dragged him out of the city, and began to stone him. The witnesses meanwhile were piling cloaks at the feet of a young man named Saul. As Stephen was being stoned he could be heard praying, "Lord Jesus, receive my spirit." He fell to his knees and cried out in a loud voice, "Lord, do not hold this sin against them," and with that he died.

From Acts 7

I like to ask the school children in my parish, "What is a martyr?" Sooner or later we get around to defining a martyr as someone who talks or teaches about Jesus and, when told to stop teaching about Jesus or face death, chooses death. The reading above recounts the story of the Church's first martyr, Stephen. Often times we think of martyrs as people who lived long ago, and while that's true, there are many modern day martyrs as well.

When the iron curtain fell in Eastern Europe in 1989, stories emerged about modern martyrs during the communist era; stories of Catholic priests, nuns and laity having been told to renounce their faith or face death or prison. Many chose death or prison. I've been thinking about those courageous people in Eastern Europe lately. I asked myself, would I go to prison or die for Christ and my faith? I'd like to think that the answer would be "yes," but then I'm not sure how I would react until I was faced with the situation. This is an academic exercise because the chances are poor that any of us will be asked to go to prison or die for Christ. However, during the course of our lives, we will feel the sting of martyrdom by getting a little taste of it now and then. I say that for two reasons: first, some of society views organized religion as a crutch, as something for the weak. Second, as Roman Catholics, we are often viewed as being out of touch with society and, therefore, can become the brunt of many jokes. We feel the sting in subtle ways. Perhaps it's the snicker or laugh at the office when we politely pass on the ham sandwich during Fridays of Lent, or maybe it's the "holy roller" comment that comes forth when we decline a Sunday morning invitation to do something because we are going to Church. That's exactly what Jesus was talking about when he said, "Blessed are you when they insult you and persecute you and slander you because of me. Rejoice and be glad for your reward in heaven will be great."

Please God, may we always have the courage, like that of St. Stephen, to stand tall and to never be ashamed to be known as one of your disciples.

When We Fail To Love

Jesus said to his disciples: "You have heard the commandment, 'you shall love your countrymen but hate your enemy.' My command to you is this: love your enemies, pray for your persecutors. This will prove that you are sons of your Heavenly Father, for His sun rises on the bad and the good, He rains on the just and the unjust. If you love those who love you, what merit is there in that? Do not tax collectors do as much? And if you greet your brothers only, what is so praiseworthy about that? Do not pagans do as much? In a word, you must be perfected as your Heavenly Father is perfect."

From Matthew 5

Humanity pays a huge price for hatred and indifference…a huge price. I was reminded of that thought recently as I read the daily newspaper. Four articles caught my attention. The first article described an Algerian car bomb that killed 17 and wounded 93. The next article described the Pope's visit to Venezuela and the Mass he celebrated with one million Venezuelan people. In his homily, the Pope blasted the political leaders for misusing and stealing the country's wealth and, therefore, leaving eight out of ten people in poverty. The third and fourth articles described the continued inability of both sides in Ireland and Yugoslavia to solve their problems peacefully. Now, as we head into a new millenium, it's sad to see that the same kinds of problems persist.

Today, we try to solve our world's problems through treaties and peace-keeping forces but they are merely bandaids on the wound. We've got to treat the actual wound to solve the problem and we can only effectively treat the wound by doing what Christ said 2000 years ago: "Love your enemies, pray for your persecutors."

Recently, I pulled up behind a car sporting a bumper sticker that read, "I don't get mad; I get even." I'm sure it was meant as a joke and yet, it's a pretty accurate description of human nature. It is easier to hate or to be indifferent than it is to love others. It is easier to hold grudges and to get even than it is to love others. Loving others is costly; it takes effort and it taxes both our emotional and financial resources. But choosing not to love others always costs more...much more.

Unexpected Changes

This is how the birth of Jesus Christ came about. When his mother Mary was engaged to Joseph, but before they lived together, she was found with child through the power of the Holy Spirit. Joseph, her husband, an upright man unwilling to expose her to the law, decided to divorce her quietly. Such was his intention when suddenly the angel of the Lord appeared in a dream and said to him: "Joseph, son of David, have no fear about taking Mary as your wife. It is by the Holy Spirit that she has conceived this child. She is to have a son and you are to name him Jesus because he will save his people from their sins."

From Matthew 1

Imagine. Can you imagine being thirteen, fourteen, maybe fifteen years old ...falling in love with someone, deciding to get married, being filled with lofty dreams, planning out your future life, and then in an instant, God comes along and dashes all your plans and hopes and in effect says, "I know what you want to do but I need you for something else. I've got different plans for you. I need you to be the parents of the Son of God."

It was in an instant that the plans, dreams and hopes of a young couple in Nazareth vanished when Mary said, "Let it be done to me as you say." Joseph, whom the angel had visited in a dream, decided not to divorce Mary because she was pregnant. This couple's decision to accept God's plan must have been based on one single thought: that they could trust God with their very lives. Even without answers to all their how and why questions, ultimate trust in God would have been the only way Mary and Joseph could have carried out what the Lord had asked of them.

God has a way of changing our plans in life too. Perhaps we have experienced the loss of a loved one, an unexpected illness, or maybe we have been the victim of corporate downsizing. Like Mary and Joseph, changes in plans can leave us stunned and full of how and why questions. Sudden changes in plans can make our future seem very scary.

Mary and Joseph ... the story of two average people who trusted their lives to God, even when their life's plan was drastically altered and they had no idea how they would accomplish the task set before them. Ultimately, God gathered them under his arm and took care of them and he will do the same for us should our life's plans change unexpectedly.

The Fruits of Our Efforts

As the messengers set off, Jesus began to speak to the crowds about John: "What did you go out to the wasteland to see – a reed swaying in the wind? Tell me, what did you go out to see – someone luxuriously dressed? Remember, those who dress luxuriously are to be found in royal palaces. Why then did you go out – to see a prophet? A prophet indeed, and something more! It is about this man that Scripture says, `I send my messenger ahead of you to prepare your way before you.' I solemnly assure you, history has not known a man born of woman greater than John the Baptizer. Yet the least born into the kingdom of God is greater than he."

From Matthew 11

Road signs... young people who are studying for their driver's permit have to learn about road signs, their different shapes and colors, and what each means to the driver. Ultimately, road signs are of great importance because they keep us going in the right direction. The role of John the Baptist was like that of a road sign; he kept the people going in the right direction as he pointed the way toward Jesus. Unfortunately, John the Baptist never got to see the fruits of his efforts; he never got to see Christ's love displayed on the cross and his rising from the dead.

Like John the Baptist we sometimes never get to see the fruits of our efforts. In our own lives, we can look back and recognize the people who acted as important road signs in our life's journey...people who helped us to stay the course or who helped us to get back onto the main road when necessary. They could be parents, siblings, a spouse, teachers, a coach, a priest or a friend...maybe even a stranger. Sometimes the people who've had a great influence on our lives never have the opportunity to see the fruits of their efforts.

I recall a dying woman telling me that her greatest regret was that her daughter had wandered far from the faith. A year or so after the woman died, her adult child asked me how she might return to the Church that she had left so many years ago. When I asked her why she was returning at this time she said that her mother's example of faithfulness was the biggest reason. The mother never lived to see the fruits of her efforts but her example provided the road signs that guided her daughter back onto the main track.

Let us never underestimate the value of giving someone a second chance, of forgiving someone who seeks our forgiveness, of taking the time to listen to a lonely voice, of reaching out and helping a stranger, or of performing random acts of kindness. Those moments may be critical road signs in someone else's life even though, like John the Baptist, we may never have the opportunity to see the fruits of our efforts in our lifetime.

A Culture of Violence

Then God said, "Let us make man in our image, after our likeness. Let them have dominion over the fish of the sea, the birds of the air, and the cattle, and over all the wild animals and all the creatures that crawl on the ground." God created man in His image; in the divine image He created him; male and female He created them.

From Genesis 1

Any successful organization or company always has fundamental principles upon which it is built. Likewise, there are certain fundamental principles upon which our faith is built. One of these principles is that all human life is special; it is sacred. Why? Because the Book of Genesis tells us that all human beings are made in the image and likeness of God. That's why our Church says over and over again: protect life in all its stages; life is sacred.

However, in our world and our American culture, people have drifted away from this fundamental principle. Increasingly, life is *not* seen as God's special gift to us. More and more, life is seen as being cheap and quite expendable. A couple of years ago, there was a story on the evening news about a fifteen-year-old who was arrested for a drive-by shooting which claimed the life of a little girl. When asked why he did it, the fifteen-year-old responded, "Because I thought it was fun." His response says "life is cheap." Think of the horror of ethnic cleansing in Kosovo… life is cheap. What about the hundreds of thousands of Africans who die each year due to disease and starvation as a result of warring factions? Life is cheap. Some years back, the mayor of Washington, D.C., asked President Clinton to deploy the National Guard because murder in our nation's capital was out of control. Again, the message is: life is cheap.

To cure the wounds of violence in our country and our world, we've got to bring back the dignity of life; the idea that life is special, that it is sacred. I don't pretend to think that the answers to the social issues I've just raised are cut and dried...very few things are today. However, as we struggle with these issues, and the issues that will surface tomorrow, may I suggest that we go back to the basics and recall that all human life is special; it is a gift from God. If we really believe that all persons are made in the image and likeness of God, we would reject our present culture of violence and conclude that love is the remedy for our social ills.

Surrendering to God

Mary set out, proceeding in haste into the hill country to a Town of Judah, where she entered Zachariah's house and greeted Elizabeth. When Elizabeth heard Mary's greeting, the baby stirred in her womb. Elizabeth was filled with the Holy Spirit, and cried out in a loud voice: "Blessed are you among women and blessed is the fruit of your womb. But who am I that the mother of my Lord should come to me? The moment your greeting sounded in my ear, the baby stirred in my womb for joy." Blessed is she who trusted that the Lord's words to her would be fulfilled.

From Luke 1

When I lived and worked in Denver, I would spend time at the Little Sisters of the Poor Nursing Home one evening each week after work. One of the little jobs that I did at the home regularly was to feed a resident by the name of Evelyn. She was a woman in her early fifties who'd been diagnosed with multiple sclerosis sometime in her mid-twenties. The disease had slowly robbed her of the use of her hands, legs, arms and even the ability to turn her head. One evening when I was feeding her, and after I had gotten to know her quite well, I said to her, "Evelyn, you're trapped in a body that won't function, yet you're so contented and at peace. How do you handle the discouragement, frustration and feeling of powerlessness that accompanies your disease?" Her response to me was, "When you have as little control over things as I do, eventually you learn to turn everything over to God and to trust God. It is then that you will find peace and contentment." I've never forgotten that bit of wisdom spoken by one of God's saints here on earth.

There is a key sentence in the visitation story concerning trusting God. It is spoken in reference to Mary: "Blessed is she who trusted." As you know, Mary's example of trust in God, a faith she kept even when she did not fully understand his plan, is one of the reasons that she is held in such high regard in our Church.

When the events of our life become confusing, burdensome, and painful, when all seems hopeless and we must endure what we cannot control, let us turn it over to God and trust that the God who created us, will also care for us, no matter what situation we face.

Anxiety

Amaziah [priest of Bethel] said to Amos, "Off with you, visionary, flee to the land of Judah! There earn your bread by prophesying, but never again prophesy in Bethel; for it is the king's sanctuary and a royal Temple. " Amos answered Amaziah, " I was no prophet, nor have I belonged to a company of prophets; I was a shepherd and a dresser of sycamores. The Lord took me from following the flock, and said to me, Go, prophesy to my people Israel.

From Amos 7

"Deal the cards." As you who are card players know, generally speaking, you're not allowed to throw in your initial hand and start over again. In most card games you have to play with the cards you've been dealt. Amos didn't like the cards he was dealt, and he wanted the deck reshuffled and dealt again. In other words, Amos didn't like the idea of being commissioned a prophet by God. He knew being commissioned a prophet by God would involve announcing a very unpopular message and so it was against his personal wish to be a prophet. He said, " I am a shepherd and a dresser of sycamores" and was very happy doing that. Yet when God called, reluctance and anxiety gave way to trust and contentment.

In Mark 6:7-13, when Jesus sent his apostles out in pairs to the neighboring towns, they were uneasy with the hand they had been dealt. They had been asked by our Lord to go on a journey and to take nothing with them-no money, no food, no clothes, a seemingly senseless thing to do. The apostles must have been tempted to say to our Lord, "Thanks for the offer, but no thanks." But, like Amos, instead of throwing down their cards, the disciple's reluctance and anxiety gave way to trust and contentment.

God has asked, and will continue to ask all of us to play some cards which we hadn't planned on being dealt. For example,

90

we may not have planned on having such a difficult time with school or with making friends, on becoming pregnant, or being widowed. Perhaps we hadn't planned on losing our jobs, finding that we have a malignant tumor, being in an auto accident or having to be in a nursing home because we've lost our ability to care for ourselves. Those are the types of cards we are sometimes dealt and we, too, are reluctant to accept them. We have the same two choices that Amos and the apostles had: 1) We can say, "God, you're responsible for this and I'm throwing in my cards; I'm checking out of the program." or 2) We can make the choice made by Amos and the apostles: "God, I don't like these cards I've been dealt, but I'll play them solely because I trust you; I trust that you will take good care of me."

Loyalty

As Jesus walked along, he saw a man who had been blind from birth. His disciples asked him, "Rabbi, was it his sin or his parents that caused him to be born blind?" "Neither," answered Jesus: "It was no sin, either of this man or of his parents. Rather, it was to let God's works show forth in him..." With that Jesus spat on the ground, made mud with his saliva, and smeared the man's eyes with the mud. Then he told him, "Go, wash in the pool of Siloam..." So the man went off and washed, and came back able to see.

From John 9

Alexander Pope once wrote: "History is more full of examples of the loyalty of dogs, than of the loyalty of friends." I saw that quote the other day and my first reaction was to think, "How sad, and how silly!" Then upon reflection, I concluded that same statement represents the thoughts of an increasing number of people. Why? Because the idea of loyalty today is not what it once was. For example, in years gone by, business deals were sealed with a handshake. Today, handshakes have been replaced with signed contracts. When professional ball players signed with a team years ago, they typically finished their careers with that same team. Now, loyalty between player and team has been replaced by economics. Perhaps where Americans have experienced diminished loyalty most acutely is in the workplace. It used to be advantageous to work for a large company; you'd be employed there until you decided to retire. In many cases today, with corporate downsizing, the loyalty that was once shared between employee and employer no longer exists. That lack of loyalty, which seems increasingly prevalent these days, affects all of us. It can cause increased stress and pain in our lives, makes it more difficult for us to trust people, and, in some cases, it can leave us feeling isolated and depressed.

The story of the man born blind is, among other things, a story of loyalty and a lack of it. The very first part of the story is represented in the passage above. But the gospel goes on to tell us, in verses 8-41, that the blind man's neighbors, the very people he grew up with, sold him out. They didn't believe his account of how he'd been healed. The Pharisees, too, sold him out. Further, they kicked him out of town. Even the blind man's parents were disloyal to him. They were afraid to answer the Pharisees' question because they thought they might be put out of the synagogue for acknowledging Jesus' miracle. Only Jesus was loyal to the blind man. Only Jesus sought him out after he was ousted from the village.

There is a lot of truth to the saying: "One who finds a loyal friend, finds a treasure." Well, Jesus Christ is a loyal friend par excellence. He will stand by us through thick and thin. He will stand by us when we've been "sold out" by others. Jesus will remain loyal to us even when we are not loyal to him.

Setting a Good Example

The Pharisees and some of the experts in the law who had come from Jerusalem gathered around Jesus. They had observed a few of his disciples eating meals without having purified--that is to say, washed--their hands. The Pharisees, and in fact all Jews, cling to the custom of their ancestors and never eat without scrupulously washing their hands. Moreover, they never eat anything from the market without first sprinkling it. There are many other traditions they observe--for example, the washing of cups and jugs and kettles. So the Pharisees and the scribes questioned him: "Why do your disciples not follow the tradition of our ancestors, but instead take food without purifying their hands?" He said to them: "How accurately Isaiah prophesied about you hypocrites when he wrote, `This people pays me lip service but their heart is far from me.'"

From Mark 7

Webster's Dictionary defines a hypocrite as one who affects virtues or qualities that he or she does not have. I like the prophet Isaiah's definition of hypocrite: a hypocrite is one who gives lip service but whose heart is far away. In Mark 7, Jesus accuses the Pharisees of being hypocrites. He tells them that in effect, they talk a good game, but that their hearts and their actions are not consistent with their words.

You probably have had the experience of someone saying to you, "I don't go to Church anymore because the people who go there are a bunch of hypocrites." I tell people who make that comment to me that we are all sinners, every human being. Hence, as Catholic Christians we're all sinners at times, those instances when we do not live up to what we profess in this Church. That's one of the reasons we really do need the Church, because the Church is for sinners and hypocrites, not so much for saints.

I have to admit that when someone says they have lost their faith or no longer attends Church because of hypocrisy, it causes me to pause and ask myself, "Have I contributed to this person's drawing that conclusion? Sometimes, I think that I have. Those moments serve as a little reminder of how loudly our actions speak as compared to our words.

I've often thought that the greatest compliment any of us could receive from a co-worker, neighbor or acquaintance is for them to say, "I've observed how you handle yourself, how you treat others, and I've concluded that you must be a follower of Jesus Christ"...what a compliment that would be!

Final Farewells

The disciples recounted what had happened on the road to Emmaus and how they had come to know Jesus in the breaking of the bread. While they were speaking about all this, he himself stood in their midst... In their panic and fright they thought they were seeing a ghost. He said to them, "Why are you disturbed? Why do such ideas cross your mind? Look at my hands and my feet; it is really I..." They were still incredulous for sheer joy and wonder, so he said to them, "Have you anything here to eat?" They gave him a piece of cooked fish, which he took and ate in their presence. Then he said to them, "Recall those words I spoke to you when I was still with you: everything written about me in the law of Moses and the prophets and psalms had to be fulfilled."

From Luke 24

"Quality time" is a term often heard in the work place and at home these days. For example, a manager might say, "We're going to spend some quality time brainstorming to determine where this company is going in the 21st century," or a parent could be heard to say, "This family is going to spend some quality time together this Sunday afternoon." Quality time refers to using time in an extremely meaningful manner.

A few years ago I had the opportunity and the privilege to be with a family as they said their good-byes to a dying loved one. That was quality time, par excellance. When we are saying our final farewell to someone we deeply love, there is no window dressing; we speak right from the heart. We get to what's important really quickly and we say only what's important.

The reading above is a story about quality time because it is Jesus' final farewell to his beloved disciples. If you look in your bible and find the 24th chapter of Luke, you'll see that there are only five lines of scripture that follow the gospel passage shown above. Those five lines describe Jesus' ascension into heaven. Of all the things that Jesus could have chosen to say in his final goodbye to his disciples, he chose to emphasize the importance of believing in his resurrection. That's why he ate the cooked fish...to show the disciples that he was not a ghost. "Look at my hands and feet," Jesus said, "it is really I." His parting message to his first disciples is the same message that Jesus gives to his disciples of today: Believe that I did rise from the dead as I promised you, and believe that someday, you also will rise.

Generosity

In the course of his teaching Jesus said: "Be on guard against the scribes, who like to parade around in their robes and accept marks of respect in public, front seats in the synagogues, and places of honor at banquets. These men devour the savings of widows and recite long prayers for appearance' sake; it is they who will receive the severest sentence." Taking a seat opposite the treasury, he observed the crowd putting money into the collection box. Many of the wealthy put in sizeable amounts; but one poor widow came and put in two small copper coins worth about a cent. He called his disciples over and told them: "I want you to observe that this poor widow contributed more than all the others who donated to the treasury. They gave from their surplus wealth, but she gave from her want, all that she had to live on."

From Mark 12

Happy people tend to be giving people. Have you found that to be the case in your own life experiences with people you've known? When I look back on the happiest, most fulfilled people in my life, co-workers, neighbors, family, and friends, they all have one common characteristic: they are (or were) giving people. They are (or were) people who had that ability to see and think beyond themselves, to reach out and invest themselves in others. They all gave a lot more of themselves than others gave them. They were counter-cultural.

What type of person do you think the poor widow was? Someday we will meet her in heaven and then we'll know for sure. Yes, she was economically poor, but I'd guess that she was also rich in happiness, contentment, and fulfillment.

A recent issue of *Time* magazine had a short article that described Americans today as less willing to give of their time and money to charitable causes. The article noted that the 1990's are often presented as a more caring decade but the proof has not been

98

found in the pudding. I'm sure there are many reasons for that phenomenon, and I'm not a sociologist, but I wonder if the growing unhappiness, anger, and general discontent that we read about everyday in this country has anything to do with Americans' growing unwillingness to share of their time, talent, and treasure with others...to give from their hearts, so to speak. I wonder if there might be a connection?

Serving Others

Jesus and his disciples came down the mountain and began to go through Galilee, but he did not want anyone to know about it ... They returned to Capernaum and Jesus, once inside the house, began to ask them, "What were you discussing on the way home?" At this they fell silent, for on the way they had been arguing about who was the most important. So he sat down and called the Twelve around him and said, "If anyone wishes to rank first, he must remain the last one of all and the servant of all." Then he took a little child, stood him in their midst, and putting his arms around him, said to them, "Whoever welcomes a child such as this for my sake welcomes me. And whoever welcomes me welcomes, not me, but him who sent me."

From Mark 9

What defines greatness? Greatness is in the eyes of the beholder. For some, greatness is an athlete who can put a round leather ball through a round metal hoop on a consistent basis. For others it is one who can lead soldiers into battle or lead a nation out of difficult times. Still for others, it is one who can evoke emotion when using a musical instrument or by stroking paint on a piece of canvas. The gospel tells us what defines greatness in the eyes of God; it is the one who dies to self-importance and who willingly serves others.

During the past year, I've made several visits to a local nursing home to help with the anointing of the sick, that beautiful sacrament which our Church has for those in need of spiritual, physical or emotional healing. One of the patients that I've visited is an elderly woman who is without the majority of her faculties. She has a beautiful smile, but she doesn't know who I am, or who anyone else is for that matter. Yet, every time I've visited, her husband has been there. One day I said to him, "You spend a great deal of time here with your wife, don't you?" He said, "Yes, Father, I do. I'm here every day, all day. You see, I never want my wife to feel as if she is alone." As I stood before him, I thought to myself, "I'm in the presence of one of the great ones in God's eyes. Here is a man dedicated in service to others, in this case, to his ailing wife."

Service to others, by definition, involves inconvenience. Service to others involves the use of our valuable time, often without many thank-you's or pats on the back, and there will be few, if any, newspaper write-ups which laud our efforts. In short, dying to self and serving others has few earthly rewards, but it certainly must put a smile on God's face...and that's reward enough.

Vocations

After John's arrest, Jesus appeared in Galilee proclaiming God's good news ... As he made his way along the Sea of Galilee, he observed Simon and his brother Andrew casting their nets into the sea; they were fishermen. Jesus said to them, "Come after me; I will make you fishers of men." They immediately abandoned their nets and became his followers. Proceeding a little farther along he caught sight of James, Zebedee's son, and his brother John. They too were in their boat putting their nets in order. He summoned them on the spot. They abandoned their father Zebedee, who was in the boat with the hired men, and went off in his company.

From Mark 1

How did the apostles first come to follow Jesus? Mark's gospel tells us the answer. It was through a verbal invitation from Jesus. He didn't wait for the apostles to come to him; no, he approached them saying, "Won't you come and follow me?"

Psychologists and sociologists tell us a lot of reasons why fewer young people are pursuing vocations as priests, brothers and sisters. There is truth to their conclusions, but sometimes I think they miss some of the most obvious reasons. To me, one reason is that we seldom verbally invite single people under the age of fifty to be sisters, brothers and priests. When was the last time you said to a young, single person, "Have you ever thought about a religious vocation? I just want you to know I think you have the gifts and talents to be a good sister, brother, or priest. We need good people like you; our Church needs good people like you."

I think that verbally inviting young people is the responsibility of all of us and I'm not sure we have done a very good job in this area. I know for myself, I was twenty-five years old before anyone verbally invited me to be a priest. Out of high school, lots of people told me they thought I'd be a good engineer

102

or teacher or whatever. But no one said anything about a vocation. For the past twenty-five years, we haven't viewed religious vocations as viable, fulfilling careers and we have to somehow change that.

Verbal invitations are a major reason I'm a priest today. Over a three to four year period while I was in my late twenties, five or six different people said in their own way, "You really ought to think about being a priest." I felt then, and I feel now, that those verbal invitations were God speaking to me through his people. Interestingly, and quite honestly, two of those six invitations came from two different women, both of whom I considered marrying. I'm not quite sure how to interpret that experience! But seriously, those verbal invitations from the two women and the other invitations were powerful experiences for me.

Pursuing a vocation doesn't take much. The only things it takes are a love for God, a big heart, and a willingness to gamble everything...to gamble everything on Jesus who said, "Won't you come and follow me?"

"Follow me."
Jn 21:19

Forgiving Others

Peter came up and asked Jesus, "Lord, when my brother wrongs me, how often must I forgive him? Seven times?" "No," Jesus replied, "not seven times; I say, seventy times seven times..."

From Matthew 18

What do you think is the single most difficult thing that Jesus has asked us to do? It would be interesting to take a survey on that question. I suspect that Jesus' command to "love one another" (including those who are unkind to us) would get a lot of votes. Jesus' command to not judge or condemn is very difficult and many would vote for that I'm sure. We've heard Jesus say, "Pick up your cross and follow me." I think that would get a lot of votes in the survey. All in all, I think that the most difficult thing Jesus has asked us to do is to forgive those who have hurt us; that would get my vote.

About thirty years ago, after the infamous prison uprising at Attica, the then governor, Nelson Rockefeller, ordered the prison to be taken back by force after inmates had held hostages for four days. In taking back the prison about forty people were killed, approximately thirty prisoners and ten staff. Twenty-five years later, the newspaper carried a series of articles in which those involved, prisoners, guards, state officials, and widows, were asked to reflect on the events that had taken place. A great majority of those interviewed still felt bitterness, anger, resentment, and even hatred toward those they felt were responsible for their pain. Even after twenty-five years, they have been unable to forgive. It's almost as though they've been walking through life for the past twenty-five years with a ball and chain wrapped around their ankles, and they just can't cut themselves free from it.

After reflecting on those newspaper articles, I felt badly for those people who'd been interviewed because hate really does destroy the one who hates and cannot forgive. Forgiveness is freeing. It allows us to move forward and to grow. It allows us to cut free the ball and chain which holds us back. Jesus doesn't expect us to forgive others overnight, especially those who have hurt us badly. Forgiveness may take years, but we are asked to try to forgive and not to savor the hate.

Our Lord stands ready to help us forgive others. As part of our morning or evening prayer, let us not be afraid to ask God for the grace to forgive those whom we find difficult to forgive. Our Lord will help us; he will give us the necessary grace.

Humans Playing God

The crowds asked John, "What ought we to do?" In reply he said, "Let the man with two coats give to him who has none. The man who has food should do the same." Tax collectors also came to be baptized, and they said to him, "Teacher, what are we to do?" He answered them, "Exact nothing over and above your fixed amount." Soldiers likewise asked him, "What about us?" He told them, "Do not bully anyone. Denounce no one falsely. Be content with your pay." The people were full of anticipation, wondering in their hearts whether John might be the Messiah. John answered them all by saying, "I am baptizing you in water, but there is one to come who is mightier than I. I am not fit to loosen his sandal strap. He will baptize you in the Holy Spirit and in fire."

From Luke 3

It's interesting to think of what some of the biblical figures will be like when we meet them in heaven. Take John the Baptist for instance. One of the traits that I think we'll find characterizes John the Baptist is humility. The gospel shows us an example of that humility. We read that many people thought that John the Baptist was the Messiah. He could have let all that go to his head; he could have taken advantage of many people. Yet, his response when asked if he was the Messiah was to say: "No, no, I am not the Messiah; he is yet to come. I am not even fit to loosen his sandal strap."

John the Baptist did not play God. Terrible things can happen when human beings attempt to play God. The names Hitler, Stalin and Mao Tse Tung come to mind when I think of people playing God. There are people who would attempt to play God today. I'll never forget a Newsweek article entitled: "Quality, Not Quantity." It is one of the saddest and most disturbing articles I have ever read about the nature of humanity.

106

The article described the Chinese government's decision to weed out or abort all inferior births for the purpose of "improving the quality of the population." Can you imagine human beings deciding that "quality" includes only those who are strong and intelligent, that only *they* have a right to live? What the Chinese government was saying is that those with physical or mental deficiencies cannot possibly have any gifts and talents to offer and, therefore, do not deserve to live. They've decided that our Lord cannot possibly reveal himself or work through a physically or mentally disabled person. God help us.

To a much lesser degree, there is a tendency in all humans to play God. We play God by judging others and by noting their weaknesses and shortcomings as opposed to their attributes. John the Baptist reminds us that our role in this life is to make ready the way of the Lord... it is not to play God.

Selflessness

Some Greeks who had come to worship at the Passover Feast came to Philip, who was from Bethsaida in Galilee, and asked him, "Sir, we would like to see Jesus." Philip went and told Andrew; then Andrew and Philip went and told Jesus. Jesus answered them, "The hour has come for the Son of Man to be glorified. Amen, amen, I say to you, unless a grain of wheat falls to the ground and dies, it remains just a grain of wheat; but if it dies, it produces much fruit.

From John 12

Jesus and Tom...these two names come to mind very quickly when I think of these words, "unless a grain of wheat falls to the ground and dies, it remains just a grain of wheat; but if it dies, it produces much fruit." I never met Tom. You see, at Seton Hall University, where I went to seminary, there is a student union on campus. As you walk into the student union, there is a plaque on the wall with about ten names on it. One of those names on the plaque is Tom; I don't recall his last name. However, I know the story about Tom that accounts for how his name got on that plaque.

Tom was a student at Seton Hall and graduated in 1968. After graduation he was drafted into the army, and after completing his training, was sent to Vietnam. One month after arriving in Vietnam, Tom was in the field with his men when an enemy grenade dropped into the midst of his platoon. Instantly, Tom threw himself on the grenade. By doing so, his body shielded his platoon members from the deadly shrapnel. Tom was a grain of wheat that died. But his death produced much fruit...the lives of the men in his platoon, all the good that those men have accomplished since that day, and all the life that has come forth from them represent the fruit of Tom's selfless act.

Jesus Christ also pounced on top of a grenade to shield all of us; Jesus pounced on the grenade of eternal death. The death of Christ has shielded us from the deadly shrapnel of eternal death. Jesus was the grain of wheat who died so that much fruit would be produced.

I doubt that a day goes by that the men in Tom's platoon don't think of him, and thank him for what he did for them. For everything that they have today is a result of a great act of selflessness. I hope that we think of Christ each day, and thank him for what he has done for us, because the eternal life that we will someday inherit and enjoy is a result of his great act of love and selflessness.

Loving Neighbor

When the Pharisees heard that Jesus had silenced the Sadducees, they assembled in a body; and one of them, a lawyer, in an attempt to trip him up, asked him, "Teacher, which commandment of the law is the greatest?" Jesus said to him: "'You shall love the Lord your God with your whole heart, with your whole soul, and with all your mind.' This is the greatest and first commandment. The second is like it: 'You shall love your neighbor as yourself.' On these two commandments, the whole law is based, and the prophets as well."

From Matthew 22

New York State law says we can't drive a car unless we are at least sixteen years old. Niagara Mohawk says we can't continue to receive power unless we have paid our bills. The gospel says we can't love God, unless we love our neighbor. In other words, loving our neighbor is a prerequisite for loving God.

Who are our neighbors? It seems to me that our neighbors fall into three categories: First would be our family and friends, those whom we love and who love us in return. It's rather easy to love these "neighbors."

A second category of neighbors would be the vast majority of the people in the world, those we don't know and with whom we have little interaction. These people have never hurt us, but they have never helped us. We love these people by treating them with respect, by not taking what doesn't belong to us or by charitable works. These "neighbors" don't inspire love based on relationships, as do those in the first category, but we find it relatively easy to respect and care for them.

The third category of neighbors would be those people we don't like. Perhaps these individuals have "burned" us in the past or have hurt us in some way...these "neighbors" are difficult to love. For those who fall into this third category, it may be helpful to remember that in all people there is inherent goodness, or God would not have created them. The catch is that with some individuals, we may have to look a little harder and a little longer to find that goodness. The key is to never give up looking.

Love one another.

Being Molded

Simon Peter, in the company of another disciple, kept following Jesus closely... The servant girl who kept the gate said to Peter, "Aren't you one of this man's followers?" "Not I," he replied... The high priest questioned Jesus, first about his disciples, then about his teaching... All through this Simon Peter had been standing there warming himself. They said to him, "Are you not a disciple of his?" He denied: "I am not!" "But did I not see you with him in the garden?" insisted one of the high priest's slaves...Peter denied it again. At that moment a cock began to crow.

From John 18

I was downtown the other day and I had my priest's collar on, when someone approached me and said, "I could never be a Catholic, because you Catholics worship saints." I responded by saying, "You have been badly misinformed somewhere along the line. Catholics do not worship saints, we worship God and God alone. We do, however, honor the saints. They hold a special place of respect in our church because of their exemplary lives." Take St. Peter, for example. Why do we honor him? Well, he was witness to the resurrection of our Lord. He was an apostle, and hence, he was one of the first teachers of the faith. Eventually, he died a martyr's death for the faith. For us, perhaps the greatest reason we honor St. Peter is because he was so very human. We can all relate to this man because he was flawed. In other words, he had human weaknesses just like you and me. In his lifetime, there were moments when he failed to trust our Lord, times he lacked courage, instances when he was unable to totally understand our Lord and moments he doubted our Lord...all the things with which we struggle.

So what was the greatness of Peter? To my mind, it was

Peter's willingness to allow our Lord to mold him into the kind of disciple Jesus wanted him to be. Our Lord took all the flaws, all the human weaknesses of Peter and, over time, molded him into something very beautiful...just like working a piece of clay. Maybe that is what we can learn from the life of Peter and all the saints; that with our willingness and cooperation, Jesus can transform our human weaknesses and flaws into something very beautiful.

Taking Time-Out

The apostles returned to Jesus and reported to him all that they had done and what they had taught. He said to them, "Come by yourselves to an out-of-the-way place and rest a little." People were coming and going in great numbers, making it impossible for them to so much as eat. So Jesus and the apostles went off in the boat by themselves to a deserted place.

From Mark 6

Time-out.   As you know, a time-out is a term used in athletic competition which designates a stoppage in play for a short period of time.   During a time-out coaches and players go to an isolated area and take a breather.   They rest themselves physically and mentally and they collect their thoughts; they review what has happened up to that point in the contest and make any adjustments if necessary.

In this passage from Mark's gospel, Jesus called a time-out. The gospel tells us that he said to his apostles, "Come by yourselves to an out-of-the way place and rest a little." Why did Jesus call a time-out?   Recall that in Mark 6:7-13 Jesus had summoned the apostles and sent them out two by two to the villages.   Now the apostles have returned from that mission.   Jesus was obviously happy to have them back and anxious to hear all about their stories and experiences.   He wanted to share in their joys and disappointments, their successes and failures.   It would be my guess that our Lord's "time-outs," those quiet times spent with his apostles, were among his most treasured moments on earth.

As busy as our Lord must have been, and by that I mean there must always have been one more person to heal or teach, he recognized the need for quiet time...quiet time not only for himself but to be with his friends.   Like our Lord, most of us are very busy. But keep in mind the idea of watching for opportunities to take time-out; time to enjoy our family, our friends, our surroundings, and above all, to enjoy our God.

Spiritual Growth

Jesus, on leaving the house on a certain day, sat down by the lakeshore. Such great crowds gathered around him that he went and took his seat in a boat while the crowd stood along the shore. He addressed them at length in parables, speaking in this fashion:

"One day a farmer went out sowing. Part of what he sowed landed on a footpath, where birds came and ate it up. Part of it fell on rocky ground, where it had little soil. It sprouted at once since the soil had no depth, but when the sun rose and scorched it, it began to wither for lack of roots. Again, part of the seed fell among thorns, which grew up and choked it. Part of it, finally, landed on good soil and yielded grain at a hundred or sixty or thirty fold."

From Matthew 13

Several weeks ago my niece and I planted some sunflower seeds. It's hard to believe, but those plants are already over three feet tall. We're going to get some nice sunflowers this fall, eight to nine inch blossoms I'd guess. Our good luck formula is simple: first, lots of water; second, good rich soil; third, frequent weeding.

In this passage from Matthew's gospel Jesus is talking about seeds, but he is not talking about sunflower seeds. The "seeds" he is referring to is God's word. Like the sunflowers, it takes three things for the seed of God's word to grow in our lives and produce abundantly. First, like the sunflower seed which grows by constantly drawing water from the soil, the seed of God's word will grow only when there is frequent communication with God. We need both individual prayer and communal prayer because that is how Jesus prayed. Second, the seed of God's word needs rich soil just like the sunflower seed. Where does God plant his seed? God plants it in the human heart.

116

The seed of God's word flourishes in a heart that is gentle and full of love, in a heart that is compassionate and merciful, in a heart that can forgive. Third, you periodically weed around sunflowers because weeds are potential seed killers. They can rob the seed of sunlight, nutrients and water. The weed that threatens to kill God's word is sin. Left unchecked, sin will kill the seed. For God's word to flourish in our lives, we've got to have the humility to recognize sin in our lives, to seek periodically God's forgiveness in the sacrament of reconciliation and to make appropriate changes.

In summary, if we pray frequently, if our hearts are full of love, and if we are willing to confront sin in our lives, then the seed of God's word will yield a hundred, or sixty, or thirty-fold within all of us.

Bargains

After the Sabbath, as the first day of the week was dawning, Mary Magdeline came with the other Mary to inspect the tomb. Suddenly, there was a mighty earthquake, as the angel of the Lord descended from Heaven. He came to the stone, rolled it back, and sat on it...the guards grew paralyzed with fear of him and fell down like dead men. Then the angel spoke, addressing the women, "Do not be frightened. I know you are looking for Jesus the crucified; he is not here. He has been raised, exactly as he promised."

From Matthew 28

Bargains...as human beings we love bargains; we love getting a good deal, don't we? Merchants know that words and phrases such as "sale", "two-for-one", or "30% off" catch the attention of consumers because these words imply a bargain. I noticed on the news the other night that great crowds were expected at a certain ski resort in Colorado. Why? Because the resort was offering free skiing for two weeks and people love bargains.

When we were baptized, Jesus Christ offered to us the greatest bargain ever known to humankind. Jesus' bargain is this: if you love me and you follow me, you too will have an Easter Sunday...you too will rise from the dead to be with me in heaven forever. What a bargain! We don't even have to be perfect in order to get in on Jesus' bargain. Jesus isn't looking for perfection from us; he's just looking for progress. Case in point: notice from the gospel reading who was the very first person to discover that Jesus had risen from the dead. It was Mary Magdeline. She was the privileged one who discovered the empty tomb. Mary Magdeline was far from perfect. She had made a lot of mistakes in her life but she turned things around for the better.

Progress, not perfection, is what our Lord seeks from us. Love God in this world and enjoy everlasting life in heaven...now there's a real bargain!

Sharing Our Faith

Jesus said to his disciples: "One who lights a lamp does not put it in the cellar or under a bushel basket, but rather on a lampstand, so that they who come in may see the light."

From Luke 11

Some years ago, a daily mass communicant told an interesting story. She related that one day at her job, a co-worker approached her and asked, "Why are you always so happy when you come to work? What puts you in such a good mood?" After thinking for a moment, the woman responded, "I think my attending Mass in the morning puts me in the right frame of mind; my faith has a lot to do with my positive outlook on life." The co-worker mused, "You know, I've been away from the Church for many years... maybe that's what I need." This interchange between the parishioner and her co-worker demonstrates that if our faith gives us joy, strength, stability and meaning in our lives, then we need to share it with others. Don't keep the light hidden under a basket, set it on a stand for all to see.

It's been my experience that there are a lot of people who are looking for something more than this world can offer and, often times, they are the very people we'd least expect. For example, I've got a good friend who I've known for many years. Faith has never played much of a role in his life. When we get together, he never asks me about my faith even though he knows how important it is to me and how much I love being a priest. This past year, to my utter amazement, he started asking me questions about faith and requested that I send him a book about it. He was looking for something more. The people we least expect are sometimes the people who are searching the most.

God is not asking us to go down to the supermarket and spout scripture. But he is saying that if faith brings something into our lives, such as joy, stability, meaning or strength, we should share it with others when the opportunity arises because there are a lot of people searching for the light that we have...so many people.

A Change of Heart

When Saul arrived back in Jerusalem he tried to join the disciples there; but it turned out that they were all afraid of him. They even refused to believe that he was a disciple. Then Barnabas took him in charge and introduced him to the disciples. He explained to them how on his journey Saul had seen the Lord, who had conversed with him, and how Saul had been speaking out fearlessly in the name of Jesus at Damascus. Saul stayed on with them, moving freely about Jerusalem and expressing himself quite openly in the name of the Lord. He even addressed the Greek-speaking Jews and debated with them. They for their part responded by trying to kill him. When the brothers learned of this, some of them took him down to Caesarea and sent him off to Tarsus.

From Acts 9

What a turnaround! The Acts of the Apostles talks about Saul, better known to us as St. Paul. For the first half of his life, he was anything but a saint, rather, he was a man who persecuted Christians. He willingly played along with the stoning death of Stephen; he constantly harassed the new Christian church by entering the houses of Christians and dragging out men and women to be jailed. Yes, Paul (Saul) was anything but a saint.

However, at about age 35, Paul experienced Jesus and subsequently converted. Christ turned his hardened, cold heart into a soft and compassionate heart. Even the disciples were leery of Paul at first, asking themselves, how can someone who was persecuting us a month ago now want to join us? They came to believe that Jesus can soften even the hardest of hearts and they watched Paul go on to become the greatest missionary in the Church.

For us, perhaps we have been hurt badly by someone with a hard heart. But remember, God can change people. God can work in people's lives to soften their hearts. However, it may take years… 10, 30, 50, maybe a lifetime. We must try not to close the door completely on those who have hurt us because with God's help, they can experience a change of heart.

A Personal Relationship With Jesus

Afterward he journeyed from one town and village to another, preaching and proclaiming the good news of the kingdom of God. Accompanying him were the Twelve and some women who had been cured of evil spirits and infirmities, Mary, called Magdalene, from whom seven demons had gone out, Joanna, the wife of Herod's steward Chuza, Susanna, and many others who provided for them out of their resources.

From Luke 8

A recent magazine article entitled, "The Evolution of Despair," noted that our modern world, even with all its technological marvels, still can be a very uncomfortable and unfulfilling place to live. The article noted that the by-products of our highly efficient lives can include any of the following: social isolation, being overwhelmed with daily commitments, unresolved anxieties, long work weeks, excessive stress and a feeling of pointlessness. The article went on to note some disturbing trends. For example, the rate of incidences of depression for people in this country has doubled over the past ten years. Suicide is the most common cause of death among young adults, after car wrecks and homicide. Finally, 15 percent of Americans suffer from clinical anxiety disorders. The article was bleak, and it expressed the joylessness, hopelessness, and meaninglessness of life as many people view it. It was a dismal way to tell the human story.

The message of Jesus Christ is a much different story. It's a story that tells us that Jesus came to rescue us from the fate described in that article. When Jesus came into this world some two thousand years ago, he brought with him gifts for all of us. His gifts include rest for the weary, daylight for the discouraged, hope for the suffering, peace for the troubled and love for the lonely. However, we will never be able to take advantage of the gifts that Jesus has offered us unless we develop a close, personal relationship with him. The apostles and the holy women, as described in the above gospel, developed a close, personal relationship with Jesus because they spent quality time with him.

Jesus stands ready to nurture a wonderful relationship with all of us but it requires our response. A relationship with Jesus takes time. It doesn't happen overnight; it takes effort, which means we will be inconvenienced at times. It will involve struggles because the journey with Jesus can sometimes be frustrating and discouraging, as the apostles and the holy women learned. However, a close, personal relationship with Jesus offers big-time paybacks on our investment. It offers hope, fulfillment, stability, peace and meaning in our lives.

Ultimately, it's a relationship that offers us eternal life and happiness in heaven.

Unanswered Prayers

As Jesus was leaving Jericho with his disciples and a sizable crowd, there was a blind beggar, Bartimaeus, sitting by the roadside. On hearing that it was Jesus of Nazareth, he began to call out, "Jesus, Son of David, have pity on me!" Many people were scolding him to make him keep quiet, but he shouted all the louder, "Son of David, have pity on me!" Then Jesus stopped and said, "Call him over"...He threw aside his cloak, jumped up, and came to Jesus. Jesus asked him, "What do you want me to do for you?" "Rabboni," the blind man said, "I want to see." Jesus said in reply, "Be on your way! Your faith has healed you." Immediately he received his sight and started to follow him up the road.

From Mark 10

Picture the scene if you will. Jesus is walking along and a large crowd is following him. Jesus stops to heal Bartimaeus and then tells him, "Be on your way." Bartimaeus chooses to join the crowd and follow Jesus. Question: Would Bartimaeus have followed our Lord if he had elected not to heal his blindness, elected not to answer his prayer as Bartimaeus had asked? I don't know. I'm not trying to take anything away from Bartimaeus but I think it would be rather easy for any of us to follow Jesus if we had just experienced a miracle. The reality of it all is that many times our requests to God are not answered in the way we asked them to be. In those cases we must ask ourselves: Do I continue to walk with the crowd who is following Jesus or do I head in the other direction?

I ran into two situations recently that spoke loudly to me. The first involved a woman in a nursing home who has been praying that she will be given the opportunity to die in her home.

The second involved a young mother who is a stroke victim. This young mother is frustrated and discouraged that her prayers for physical healing have not been granted and she is experiencing the depths of depression. In both cases, it appears that they will not have the same miraculous healing that Bartimaeus had. But, despite their discouragement, both of these women have decided to pick up their crosses, the cross of old age and the cross of being disabled, and follow Christ. They could have gone in another direction, but they have chosen to trust our Lord and follow him up the steep hill. These two women have taught me what faith is all about; they have been the teachers and I have been the student.

I have no doubt that Bartimaeus is in heaven with our Lord but I also have no doubt that when we hoist the cross of unanswered prayers upon our backs and freely choose to follow Christ, that he will have special words for us when we finish the journey, words similar to these: "My child, you had every reason not to follow me. Yet you trusted me and you walked with me. Well done good and faithful servant, the Kingdom of God is yours."

Conflict

As the Jewish Passover was near, Jesus went up to Jerusalem. In the temple precincts he came upon people engaged in selling oxen, sheep, and doves, and others seated changing coins. He made a [kind of] whip of cords and drove them all out of the temple area, sheep and oxen alike, and knocked over the moneychangers' tables, spilling their coins. He told those who were selling doves, "Get them out of here! Stop turning my Father's house into a marketplace!" ...At this the Jews responded, "What sign can you show us authorizing you to do these things?" "Destroy this temple," was Jesus' answer, "and in three days I will raise it up." ...Actually he was talking about the temple of his body. Only after Jesus had been raised from the dead did his disciples recall that he had said this, and come to believe the Scripture and the word he had spoken.

From John 2

Jesus is in the midst of conflict. We can feel the conflict if we visualize the above reading. Two thoughts come to mind when I visualize the scene in the temple.

First, note that Jesus didn't allow himself to be taken advantage of by the merchants and moneychangers. They were desecrating the temple and Jesus called them to accountability for their actions. Our faith does not include a calling for us to be walked on or taken advantage of in the real world. We can still be the loving, forgiving and compassionate people Jesus has called us to be without being a doormat for people to walk on.

Second, there is no question that most anger is harmful. We need only to watch the news or read the newspaper to see the destruction caused to society as a result of unhealthy anger. However, I would offer to you that there is such a thing as "healthy anger." There are times when anger can be justified and today's

128

reading is one such example. Jesus is angry, a side of our Lord that we don't see often, but he expresses a "healthy anger" because individuals are not respecting the sacredness of the temple. Occasionally, we hear Pope John Paul II express "healthy anger" when he speaks of war, poverty and other tragic conditions occurring throughout the world. Occasionally, anger can be healthy, especially if we believe that the actions we observe would anger even Jesus himself.

All Saints

When Jesus saw the crowds he went up on the mountainside. After he had sat down, his disciples gathered around him, and he began to teach them:
"How blest are the poor in spirit: the reign of God is theirs. Blest too are the sorrowing; they shall be consoled...Blest are they who hunger and thirst for holiness; they shall have their fill. Blest are they who show mercy; mercy shall be theirs... Blest too the peacemakers; they shall be called children of God. Blest are those persecuted for holiness' sake; the reign of God is theirs. Blest are you when they insult you and persecute you and utter every kind of slander against you because of me. Be glad and rejoice, for your reward in Heaven is great".

From Matthew 5

The history of why we celebrate the Feast of All Saints on November first is an interesting one. Before Christianity came to Ireland, the pagans believed that everyone who died in the past year would assemble on October thirty-first to choose the body of the person they would inhabit for the next twelve months, before they could pass peacefully into the afterlife. To frighten off any roving souls, Celtic family members dressed themselves as demons, ghosts, goblins and witches on October thirty-first. Once Christianity was introduced in Ireland, there was a need to counter this pagan feast of Halloween and so, November first was chosen as the Feast of All Saints.

The beatitudes nicely define saints both past and present. The beatitudes tell us:

Blessed are the poor in spirit and the sorrowing. Saints are not exempt from suffering. They know what it is to experience loss, pain and disappointment. Saints are asked to pick up their crosses and follow Christ without knowing the answers to the "why" questions.

Blessed are those who hunger for holiness. Saints want to be like Christ, yet they are sinners. However, saints are sinners who keep trying. Saints are not satisfied with the status quo. They motivate themselves to try to do better.

Blessed are those who show mercy. Saints don't take advantage of others. They are sensitive to individuals' needs and are motivated to alleviate other people's pain.

Blessed are the peacemakers. Saints are gentle people. They frequently use phrases such as "I'm sorry," "I forgive you," or "it's my fault." Saints work a little harder to find the good in people rather than the more obvious shortcomings.

Blessed are they who are persecuted in the name of Christ. Saints know what it's like to be snickered at on the ball field or called a "holy roller" at work. Saints know the rejection that occurs when they refuse to follow the crowd. They don't buy into the popular cliché, "But everybody does it."

In short, saints, both past and present, are those who let the light of Christ shine through them.

Social Problems

Love is patient; Love is kind. Love is not jealous, it does not put on airs, it is not snobbish. Love is never rude, it is not self-seeking, it is not prone to anger; neither does it brood over injuries. Love does not rejoice in what is wrong, but rejoices with the truth. There is no limit to love's forbearance, to its trust, its hope, its power to endure...There are in the end three things that last: faith, hope, and love, and the greatest of these is love.

From 1 Corinthians 12 and 13

Have you ever noticed that it's sometimes easier to define a term by identifying what it is not, rather than what it is? Such is the case as St. Paul struggles to define love. Paul starts off by telling us what love is; it is patient and kind. Then he shifts gears and seems to find it easier to define love by identifying what it is not. Paul tells us that love is not jealous, haughty, snobbish or rude; it is not vengeful, selfish, or prone to anger.

Recently, I flipped through the front section of our local newspaper and jotted down topics, contained in the articles found there, which violate Paul's definition of love. In only eight pages, I found the following topics: murder, scandal, starvation, abortion, war, cheating, lying, stealing, assault, kidnapping, and need for control. All those issues are a result of humanity's failure to love; so much pain and suffering results when the law of love is violated.

I'm sure sociologists would argue it's not that simple, that the problems and woes of the world in general, and of our society in particular, are more complex than simply a failure to love. However, it seems to me that humanity's failure to love, as Paul defined love, is the root of a great majority of our social ills today. I sometimes think that God must be sitting in heaven, shaking his head and saying to himself, "I gave them the tool for happiness when I gave them the ability to love, but they have chosen not to fully embrace it."

Dormant Faith

Jesus said to the crowd: "This is how it is with the reign of God. A man scatters seed on the ground. He goes to bed and gets up day after day. Through it all the seed sprouts and grows without his knowing how it happens. The soil produces of itself first the blade, then the ear, finally the ripe wheat in the ear. When the crop is ready he 'wields the sickle, for the time is ripe for harvest."'

He went on to say: What comparison shall we use for the reign of God? ... It is like a mustard seed which, when planted in the soil, is the smallest of all the earth's seeds, yet once it is sown, springs up to become the largest of shrubs.

From Mark 4

Basil and asparagus...I love both of them but what different growing patterns they have! It takes only about three days for basil to germinate. You don't have to wait long to see the fruits of your efforts. Asparagus on the other hand takes three years from the time you plant it until you get something you can eat. During those three years you have to nurture the asparagus; you have to weed it, water it, and fertilize it, and you get nothing for your efforts during this period.

The seed of faith is similar to that of the basil and the asparagus. I say that because the seed of faith is planted in us at baptism. For some people it doesn't take long for the seed to germinate, to grow and to produce much fruit...like the basil. For others, it takes a long time for the seed planted by God at baptism to emerge and to produce...that's like the asparagus.

When we have family members or friends who fall into that second category it can be painful and discouraging waiting for the seed to germinate. Sometimes parents, spouses, and siblings of the individuals ask themselves, "What did I do wrong?" and "Did the seed planted in my loved one at baptism ever take root, or has it died?" In those cases, we must continue to nourish the seed even though nothing seems to happen...like the asparagus.

We can nourish dormant baptismal seeds in others in many ways: by our living out the commandments and the beatitudes, by sharing what our faith means to us, maybe through issuing a gentle invitation to join us in prayer or at Mass, and by praying for those whose baptismal seeds have not yet sprouted. There are many ways in which we can cultivate and nourish God's dormant seed in others, but we can only nourish the seed. Only God and the individual can make the seed grow. God will choose when and how the seed will grow. Maybe germination of the seed in someone we love won't take place until after we have died; maybe we will never see the fruits of our efforts. Maybe God will choose a period of sickness or confusion as the time for growth to begin in a person. But the thing to keep in mind is this: trust God, be patient with God and continue to cultivate and nourish the dormant baptismal seeds in those people around us, even though there appears to be no fruit.

God-Given Talents

Jesus told this parable to his disciples: "A man was going on a journey. He called in his servants and handed his funds over to them according to each man's abilities...Then he went away. Immediately the man who received the five thousand went to invest it and made another five. In the same way the man who received the two thousand doubled his figure. The man who received the thousand went off instead and dug a hole in the ground, where he buried his master's money. After a long absence, the master of those servants came home and settled accounts with them. The man who had received the five thousand came forward bringing an additional five...his master said to him, `Well done! You are an industrious and reliable servant...' The man who had received the two thousand then stepped forward. `My lord,' he said, `You entrusted me with two thousand and I have made two thousand more.' His master said to him, `Cleverly done! You, too, are an industrious and reliable servant... Come, share your master's joy!' Finally, the man who had received the thousand stepped forward. `My lord,' he said, `I knew you were a hard man... so out of fear I went off and buried your thousand silver pieces in the ground. Here is your money back.' His master exclaimed, [`You wicked and lazy slave!']...`You there! Take the thousand away from him and give it to the man with the ten thousand...throw this worthless servant into the darkness outside, where he can wail and grind his teeth.'"

From Matthew 25

Everyone has God-given talents, those gifts which make each and every one of us special in our own right. There are the obvious gifts and talents that we see in people...things like natural intelligence, athleticism, perhaps outstanding musical or mechanical ability. There are also less obvious gifts and talents given to us by God; I call them the gifts and talents of the heart.

136

These gifts are things like patience, humility, courage, compassion, and kindness. No one is without gifts and talents. Granted, some people seem to have more than others and it is natural for us to wish that we had certain natural abilities that we don't have. However, God has given each of us the necessary gifts and talents that we need to carry out the unique life mission that he has planned for us. The question is, what do we do with the unique gifts and talents given to us by God? Do we use our special abilities and attributes to serve God and our fellow human beings, or do we waste or misuse our gifts and talents?

In the parable above, the first two servants wisely invested their money and doubled their number of silver pieces. For this they were praised by their master. The first two servants represent people who use their natural abilities to build up the Kingdom of God and to make this earth a little more Christ-like. The third servant, however, buried his silver pieces rather than investing them. Eventually, he is chastised by his master. The third servant represents those who squander or misuse their gifts and talents.

It is worth remembering that all of the gifts and talents we have are God-given; we have done nothing to deserve them or to earn them. However, God does expect us to put our gifts and talents to good use, to do what we can to build up the Kingdom of God here on earth.

God in the Midst of Suffering

Job spoke, saying: Is not man's life on Earth a drudgery? Are not his days those of a hireling? He is a slave who longs for the shade, a hireling who waits for his wages. So I have been assigned months of misery, and troubled nights have been told of for me.

If in bed I say, "When shall I arise?" then the night drags on; I am filled with restlessness until the dawn. My days are swifter than a weaver's shuttle; they come to an end without hope. Remember that my life is like the wind; I shall not see happiness again.

From Job 7

Can any good come from suffering? That question comes to mind when we read the above passage from Job, a man filled with sorrow and hopelessness. In our Catholic tradition we would say "yes," good can come from suffering. Why? Because suffering is one of the ways that God speaks to us at a deep and intimate level. The concept of suffering as one means through which God enters our lives came alive for me a few years ago.

For a period of two months, I visited a man in the hospital who was seriously ill and physically suffering a great deal. The first time I met him it was very clear to me that he was bitter at either God, the Church, priests or some combination thereof. In the following weeks, his condition worsened and my visits with him became less than one minute long. During those short visits I would say a few prayers and assure him that others were praying for him at the Church. He said nothing and refused to make eye contact with me. However, about the tenth time I saw him, the last time I saw him, he was a different person. There was contentment in his eyes; he was happy to see me. The man made the sign of the

138

cross, he clutched my hands and he indicated that he wanted to say more prayers. I wanted to ask him what had happened but the man had tubes in his mouth and he couldn't speak. Clearly, something had taken place between God and that man. He died three days later so I never found out what had happened. Whatever it was, I'm sure it was something very beautiful. I really believe that for that man, suffering was redemptive; it was the means by which God called him back to himself. I saw this as a wonderful example of how God can work in the midst of suffering, having had the opportunity to see firsthand that good can come from such suffering.

In conclusion, please understand that I'm not saying God works in the midst of all suffering for all people, nor am I saying that we should be looking for opportunities to suffer. However, I do think that the saints and great spiritual writers throughout the centuries were on to something when they said in reference to suffering: "We experience the power of God only when we have experienced our own powerlessness."

The Mercy of God

The tax collectors and sinners were all gathered around to hear Jesus, at which the Pharisees and the scribes murmured, "This man welcomes sinners and eats with them." Then he addressed this parable to them: "Who among you, if he has a hundred sheep and loses one of them, does not leave the ninety-nine in the wasteland and follow the lost one until he finds it? And when he finds it, he puts it on his shoulders in jubilation. Once arrived home, he invites friends and neighbors in and says to them, 'Rejoice with me because I have found my lost sheep.' I tell you, there will likewise be more joy in Heaven over one repentant sinner than over ninety-nine righteous people who have no need to repent."

From Luke 15

The Parable of the Lost Sheep reminds me of a true story told to me by a Holy Cross priest while I was in the seminary. This priest was a prisoner of war in Bangladesh during World War II. During the one year of his imprisonment, two hundred of the two thousand prisoners died of starvation. The starvation was not due to a lack of food; rather, it was because of a cold-hearted Japanese officer. This particular Japanese officer would allow edible food to rot outside the prison fence instead of giving it to the prisoners. The priest told of how he and another captured Catholic chaplain would celebrate Mass for the other prisoners. The priest had a small container of wine and an eyedropper. He would take one drop of wine, place it in a small cup, and that would be his chalice. The Japanese would watch curiously as the prisoners celebrated the Mass.

Shortly after the war, the other priest who had been a prisoner in that camp was playing golf in the Philippines. He noticed that the man golfing in front of him had a distinctive limp; it was the Japanese officer who had starved the two hundred prisoners. The priest reported the man to the authorities. Subsequently, the Japanese officer was arrested, tried, found guilty of war crimes and sentenced to death.

The evening before his execution, the former Japanese officer requested to see the priest who had spotted him on the golf course. The priest came and the former Japanese officer asked him to explain the Mass that he'd seen celebrated in the prison years ago. The priest explained the Mass and ultimately spent the whole night with this man teaching him about the Catholic faith. The next morning the Japanese officer was baptized, confirmed and received the eucharist. The priest escorted the man to the gallows and the convicted man's last words before dying were, "I am guilty of the crimes for which I am about to die and am heartily sorry for my actions but I am excited about meeting the God that I learned about last night."

There is no question in my mind that the Japanese officer is in heaven with God today. Why? Because our God is full of mercy and forgiveness. We need only to bring to him a heart that is humble, honest, and sorrowful.

Material Possessions

As Jesus was setting out on a journey a man came running up, knelt down before him and asked, "Good Teacher, what must I do to share in everlasting life? Jesus answered, "Why call me good? No one is good but God alone. You know the commandments..." He replied, "Teacher, I have kept all these since my childhood." Jesus looked at him with love and told him, "There is one thing more you must do. Go and sell what you have and give to the poor; you will then have treasure in Heaven...At these words the man's face fell. He went away sad, for he had many possessions. Jesus looked around and said to his disciples, "How hard it is for the rich man to enter the kingdom of God!"

From Mark 10

After reading the passage from Mark's gospel, one might conclude that our Lord begrudges us having money, material possessions, a good job, or perhaps good fortune. This is not so. Our Lord does not begrudge us having any of those things but I think we need to add two qualifiers to the thought.

First, there is little doubt that our Lord expects us to share our resources and our good fortune with those less fortunate than ourselves. That was a main message that Pope John Paul II had for the people of Brazil during his 1997 visit to their country...that the "haves" must share their resources with the "have-nots". Therefore, with good fortune comes responsibility; we are called upon to share with those in need, however we may choose to do so.

Second, our Lord does not detest the fact that we have money or material resources, but would detest the idea of our falling in love with money or material resources.

On that note I am reminded of an old Russian folk tale about a peasant couple who, after each evening meal, would say, "If only we had enough land, then we would be happy." As time went on, the couple acquired more and more land, but the evening meal always ended with the same complaint: "If only we had enough land, then we would be happy." Eventually, the couple did acquire a great deal of land and became wealthy landowners.

One day a king came to the couple's house for dinner and when the meal ended they again said, "If only we had enough land, then we would be happy." To this the king asked, "How much land is enough?" The man responded that all the land he could encircle on foot in one day would be enough. The king invited him to his estate and told the man he could have all the land he could encompass, provided he was back by sunset. At the crack of dawn the man started out. He ran, then walked when he was tired, always widening his circle to gain more land. Near the end of the day, the man could see his wife and the king in the distance. Instead of heading straight for them, he decided to make a little larger circle in order to encompass the magnificent home of the king. Just as the sun set, the man reached his wife and the king. Victorious, he laughed, and then he died. You see, his overworked heart had failed him. The man was buried the next day.

How much land was enough? A plot three feet wide, by seven feet long, by six feet deep. That is what all of us will have in the end.

Fear

Jesus said to his Apostles: "Do not let men intimidate you. Nothing is concealed that will not be revealed, and nothing hidden that will not become known. What I tell you in darkness, speak in the light. What you hear in private, proclaim from the housetops."

"Do not fear those who deprive the body of life but cannot destroy the soul. Rather, fear him who can destroy both body and soul in Gehenna. Are not two sparrows sold for next to nothing? Yet not a single sparrow falls to the ground without your Father's consent. As for you, every hair on your head has been counted; so do not be afraid of anything.

From Matthew 10

In 1932, Franklin Roosevelt said, "The only thing we have to fear is fear itself." I thought of FDR's famous line because Jesus speaks of fear in Matthew's gospel. Fear is a part of all of our lives, isn't it? Fear comes in many forms. Maybe it's the fear of losing one's job. Maybe it's the fear of failure, for example, failure as a parent or as a husband or wife. Maybe it's a fear of failure in school, be it academically, athletically, or socially. Perhaps it is a fear of losing some aspect of our health, such as the loss of our mind, our mobility, or our freedom to live independently. Fear is something we all must deal with at certain times in our lives.

This past week I was talking to a young man who is about my age. He is a very faithful man who is slowly going blind from a genetic disorder. He fears blindness as any of us would. This man asked me, "What spiritual guidance can you offer me?" I almost felt guilty offering him any advice because I had not walked in his shoes. I said to him, "All I can tell you is what Jesus said in the scriptures; He said, 'As for you, every hair on your head has been counted, so do not be afraid of anything.'"

If Jesus were here today, I think he would change FDR's famous line to read as follows: "If you believe in me, and if you have faith in me, then no matter what happens, the only thing you have to fear is fear itself."

Have no fear.

Making a Difference

After Jesus' birth in Bethlehem of Judea during the reign of King Herod, astrologers from the east arrived one day in Jerusalem inquiring, "Where is the newborn king of the Jews? We observed his star at its rising and have come to pay him homage..." Herod called the astrologers aside and found out from them the exact time of the star's appearance...After their audience with the king, they set out. The star which they had observed at its rising went ahead of them until it came to a standstill over the place where the child was. They were overjoyed at seeing the star, and on entering the house, found the child with Mary, his mother. They prostrated themselves and did him homage. Then they opened their coffers and presented him with gifts of gold, frankincense, and myrrh.

From Matthew 2

Every year I'm fortunate to receive many wonderful Christmas cards. I read those cards carefully because every year they give me the basis of my Christmas homily and my Epiphany homily. One card that stood out to me asked this question: "What gifts shall we bring to celebrate Jesus' birth?" The answer written was "Love in every heart and peace on earth."

I love the story of the wise men bringing gifts to the Christ child...gifts of gold, frankincense, and myrrh. How about us; what gifts do we bring to Jesus? I can think of no two gifts that would be more meaningful to our Lord than love in every heart, and peace on earth. However, when we think about that for a moment, reality hits us. We look at the newspapers and all the human sickness jumps out at us: selfishness, greed, misuse of power, starvation, war, murder, corruption, etc. It can leave us feeling overwhelmed and we ask ourselves, "What can I do as an individual when these problems are so big, so beyond my control?

That feeling of being overwhelmed can lead us to almost withdraw from the world, to crawl into our safe cocoon and say, "I'm going to take care of myself and my family and I'll let the world fend for itself."

Love in every heart and peace on earth...we can't give those two gifts to our Lord by withdrawing from the world. True, all those problems I mentioned are bigger than we are but we can do something about the little part of the world we do affect. Edward Hale once put this idea much more eloquently than I ever could. He said:

I am only one
But still I am one
 I cannot do everything
But I can do something
 And because I cannot do everything
I will not refuse to do
 The something that I can do

Love in every heart and peace on earth...two wonderful gifts to give to our Lord.

Christic the King

Pilate said to Jesus, "Are you the king of the Jews?" Jesus answered, "Are you saying this on your own, or have others been telling you about me?" "I am no Jew!" Pilate retorted. "It is your own people and the chief priests who have handed you over to me. What have you done?" Jesus answered, "My kingdom does not belong to this world. If my kingdom were of this world, my subjects would be fighting to save me from being handed over to the Jews. As it is, my kingdom is not here." At this Pilate said to him, "So then, you are a king?" Jesus replied, "It is you who say I am a king. The reason I was born, the reason why I came into the world, is to testify to the truth. Anyone committed to the truth hears my voice."

From John 18

Following the Gulf War, one of the most sought after speakers in this country was General Norman Schwartzkopf. The commander of the coalition forces in Kuwait returned from the Gulf War to find that much of America was intrigued with him because he seemed to be a different type of general. He was different from what we had been accustomed to seeing in a combat leader. Here was a man who seemed to have great love and affection for his soldiers. He was a commander who insisted that his officers eat in the rain if their enlisted soldiers must do so. He was a general who stated that minimizing enemy casualties was a major factor in his tactical decision-making process. Norman Schwartzkopf intrigued America because he was a different type of general.

In celebrating "Christ the King" we see that Jesus Christ is and was a different type of king. When we think of an earthly king we envision a crown of gold, but Christ the King wore a crown of thorns. Most earthly kings dine only with royalty, but Christ the

148

King dined with sinners, tax collectors, the sick and the forgotten. Earthly kings had servants wash their feet, but Christ the King washed the feet of his disciples. Earthly kings imprison those who reject them, but Christ the King forgives seventy times seven times those who reject him. Earthly kings desire power; Christ the King said to be careful of power. Earthly kings have been heard to say, "destroy them"; Christ the King said, "love them." Most earthly kings are not in touch with the common folk; Christ the King knows us better than we know ourselves. Earthly kings love to be served; Christ the King came to serve others. Most earthly kings have hearts full of pride; Christ the King advocates hearts full of humility. Earthly kings are intent on building up their riches, yet Christ the King said, "share your riches." Earthly kings often use intimidation to get their point across; Christ the King uses gentleness to get his point across.

When you and I meet Jesus someday, we will indeed meet a king, but don't expect him to act like an earthly king, dress like one or talk like one. Christ the King will be a drastically different type of king.

The Joyful Jesus

There was a wedding at Cana in Galilee, and the mother of Jesus was there. Jesus and his disciples had likewise been invited to the celebration. At a certain point the wine ran out and Jesus' mother told him, "They have no more wine." Jesus replied, "Woman, how does this concern of yours involve me? My hour has not yet come." His mother instructed those waiting on table, "Do whatever he tells you..." "Fill those jars with water," Jesus ordered, at which they filled them to the brim. "Now," he said, "draw some out and take it to the waiter in charge." They did as he instructed them. The waiter in charge tasted the water made wine, without knowing where it had come from... Then the waiter in charge called the groom over and remarked to him..."What you have done is to keep the choice wine until now." Jesus performed this first of his signs at Cana in Galilee.

From John 2

First impressions are so important, aren't they? They're often lasting impressions. Whether it's a coach watching a player for the first time, a teacher's initial observation of a student, a boss evaluating a new employee, or someone sizing up the new next door neighbor, first impressions are lasting impressions.

At Cana, Jesus made a powerful first impression. You see, the miracle at Cana, where Jesus turned the water into wine, was his very first miracle. Note that it was a miracle performed in the midst of a celebration, a time of great joy. In the time of Jesus, life was hard and monotonous. There was little in which to rejoice. When there was a wedding, therefore, everyone participated in the celebration. The bride and groom would typically be married on the third day of the week (Tuesday) because that was the day of double blessings. They would then proceed through the village streets and everyone would come out to offer their congratulations. Then people would follow the couple to their new house where the newlyweds would host a party, an open house, for seven days. Further, the Jewish symbol of joy and happiness was wine and so it was expected that there would be plenty of wine over those seven days. It would have been a great embarrassment for the groom to run out of wine and so Jesus, without telling the groom, miraculously changed the water into wine.

Early in his ministry, Jesus made a powerful statement with his first miracle because that miracle took place in the midst of a celebration. Many of the miracles Jesus performed, such as the healing of the sick, the cleansing of those possessed, and the raising of the dead, were performed during times of great sadness. We've always known that Jesus is with us in times of despair, but here we see that he is also present in times of great joy and happiness. When we are rejoicing with family and friends at the peak moments of our lives, our Lord is present in our celebration. This is a God who loves to be in our midst when we are joyful and happy.

Temptation

Jesus was led into the desert by the Spirit to be tempted by the devil. He fasted forty days and forty nights, and afterward was hungry. The tempter approached and said to him, "If you are the Son of God, command these stones to turn into bread." Jesus replied, "Scripture has it: `Not on bread alone is man to live but on every utterance that comes from the mouth of God.'" Next the devil took him to the holy city, set him on the parapet of the temple, and said, "If you are the Son of God, throw yourself down. Scripture has it: `He will bid his angels take care of you; with their hands they will support you that you may never stumble on a stone.'" Jesus answered him, "Scripture also has it: `You shall not put the Lord your God to the test.'" The devil then took him to a lofty mountain peak and displayed before him all the kingdoms of the world in their magnificence, promising, "All these will I bestow on you if you prostrate yourself in homage before me." At this, Jesus said to him, "Away with you, Satan! Scripture says: `You shall do homage to the Lord your God; him alone shall you adore.'" At that the devil left him and angels came and waited on him.

From Matthew 4

Temptation to sin is a part of all of our lives. Eve, in the garden, was unable to resist the temptation to eat from the forbidden tree. In contrast to Eve's experience, when Jesus was faced with the devil's tempting, he was able to resist. Notice a subtle, but very important difference in the two stories: Jesus was in prayer when he said "no" to temptation, but in Eve's story, there is no mention of her being in prayer. There is a connection between prayer and resisting the temptation to sin. The fact that we pray regularly is no guarantee that we will never be swayed by temptation, but it sure can help a lot. It's like catching a cold. The fact that we may eat a balanced diet, exercise regularly, and get

152

plenty of sleep doesn't guarantee that we won't catch cold. But it can make it less likely because we've done some things to build up our resistance.

For me, when I'm finding time for prayer every day, quality one-on-one communication with God, resisting temptation is not difficult. When I fail to resist the temptation to sin, I can almost always trace it back to the fact that I've been cheating on my daily prayer life; that's almost always the case for me. Even though I might be doing good things with the time that I would normally be using for prayer, it still catches up to me.

We are called to come to grips with temptation and sin in our lives. The first step in accomplishing that goal is to establish or re-establish that quality daily prayer life. The type of prayer is not important, the duration of the prayer is not that important, but doing it every day and making it quality prayer is important.

Pride and Self Righteousness

As he moved on, Jesus saw a man named Matthew at his post where taxes were collected. He said to him, "Follow me." Matthew got up and followed him. Now it happened that, while Jesus was at table in Matthew's home, many tax collectors and those known as sinners came to join Jesus and his disciples at dinner. The Pharisees saw this and complained to his disciples, "What reason can the Teacher have for eating with tax collectors and those who disregard the law?" Overhearing the remark, he said: "People who are in good health do not need a doctor; sick people do. Go and learn the meaning of the words, 'It is mercy I desire and not sacrifice.' I have come to call, not the self-righteous, but sinners."

From Matthew 9

I was thinking this week about how much pressure society places on each of us...indirect, but subtle pressure from all sides to conform to things that are often contrary to what Jesus has asked us to do. Consumerism is one such example. When we read the Sunday newspaper, two-thirds of the paper are ads inviting us to buy something. The underlying, repetitive message is that if we buy the product, it will make us happy. We'll hear the same message on billboards, television, radio and in magazines.

Another example of a subtle, yet powerful societal pressure is unhealthy pride or self righteousness. It is very fashionable today to have an exaggerated sense of self...to have an overly high opinion of one's self. But we pay a tremendous price when we buy into unhealthy pride and self righteousness. It's harmful in our personal relationships because nothing is ever our fault. It's always someone else's fault...his fault, her fault, anyone else's fault but my fault. Likewise, unhealthy pride and self righteousness damage our relationship with God because we no

154

longer recognize sin in our lives…we always have an excuse for God.

In the above scriptural passage from Matthew, the Pharisees were full of unhealthy pride and self-righteousness…they couldn't understand why Jesus would eat with such "low-lifes". But Jesus sharply rebuked the Pharisees. This is but one scriptural passage where Jesus urges us to rid ourselves of unhealthy pride and self-righteousness. Why? Because left unchecked, unhealthy pride and self-righteousness can destroy us and the relationships we value most.

Baptism

Jesus said to the crowd, "The reign of God is like a buried treasure which a man found in a field. He hid it again, and rejoicing at his find, went and sold all he had and bought that field. Or again, the Kingdom of Heaven is like a merchant's search for fine pearls. When he found one really valuable pearl, he went back and put up for sale all that he had and bought it."

From Matthew 13

Matthew's gospel, chapter 13, speaks of a treasure, a great treasure. The scripture passage makes me think of all the children who are about to be baptized into the faith this day. Symbolically speaking, each of those children will be given a great treasure by God. As adults, we have already received the treasure through our own baptism. Everyone is entitled to the treasure, be they tall or short, white or black, rich or poor; everyone gets the same treasure. We are all asked to safeguard the treasure throughout our life's journey, to keep a firm grasp on it, to make it a top priority in life. No person can ever take the treasure from us; it's a personal gift from God. However, we can freely choose to abandon the treasure given to us by God. As we walk through life this God-given treasure can become heavy and inconvenient. People might even laugh at us because of the way in which we value the treasure. At times we lack the wisdom of Solomon and we make foolish and unwise choices. We rid ourselves of God's treasure and begin to embrace other earthly treasures, things that look attractive from the outside. As attractive as earthly treasures may seem, they can offer only short-term payoffs and pleasures. By embracing the earthly treasures, we run the risk of losing God's treasure.

In this parable the man gave up everything to get the treasure. But we already have the treasure and so we must do everything we can to protect it. At the end of our lives we will open up the treasure given to us by God. Do you know what we'll find in the treasure if we carry it throughout our lives? A one-way ticket to heaven and an invitation to live with God forever. Now *that's* a treasure worth giving up everything for.

Bread and Wine

I received from the Lord what I handed on to you, namely, that the Lord Jesus on the night in which he was betrayed took bread, and after he had given thanks, broke it and said, "This is my body, which is for you. Do this in remembrance of me." In the same way, after the supper, he took the cup, saying, "This cup is the new covenant in my blood. Do this, whenever you drink it, in remembrance of me." Every time, then, you eat this bread and drink this cup, you proclaim the death of the Lord until he comes!

From 1 Corinthians 11

Why do you think Jesus chose bread and wine for the Last Supper? Do you think the bread and wine were arbitrary? No, Jesus chose those elements because they had real meaning to the people of his time. For example, in the Old Testament, bread was considered a source of sustenance and, in the lives of people two thousand years ago, bread was essential to life; it was the staple of one's diet.

Wine, in the Old Testament, was the symbol of God's bountiful grace and thus, wine was seen as a symbol of joy and celebration. As you remember, in the story of the wedding at Cana, Jesus turned the water into wine because it was a day of great celebration.

Through the meaning of bread and wine, Jesus defines for us what the Eucharist is. It is our sustenance, our strength for the week ahead and it is our joy…the joy that comes from knowing we are a member of God's family and heirs to eternal life in heaven.

The Our Father

[Jesus said], "This is how you are to pray: Our Father in Heaven, hallowed be your name, your kingdom come, your will be done, on earth as in Heaven. Give us today our daily bread; and forgive us our debts, as we forgive our debtors; and do not subject us to the final test, but deliver us from the evil one. If you forgive others their transgressions, your Heavenly Father will forgive you. But if you do not forgive others, neither will your Father forgive your transgressions."

From Matthew 6

If we could combine the number of times that all of us have recited the Our Father throughout the course of our lives we'd have a big number; it would be thousands upon thousands of times. As you know, when we recite something as many times as we have recited the Our Father, sometimes we don't think about the meaning of the words. Recently, I was reflecting on the words that make up the Our Father, the words that Jesus taught his disciples, and two things struck me. First is the importance our Lord places on forgiving others as he has forgiven us. Second is our Lord's expectation that we will trust him as expressed in the phrase, "your will be done."

In my opinion, those are the two most difficult callings of a Christian...forgiving those who have hurt us and trusting God when tragedy or uncertainty strikes; those two things can seem nearly impossible for us to accomplish. However, may I suggest the "tiny step" approach to attaining these goals. Forgiving others and trusting God are not going to come overnight. But, if each week or month we can take a tiny step in the right direction, we can get on the right track. Those tiny steps happen by asking God each day for the grace to forgive others and to trust him, and God always gives us the graces we ask for. Many tiny little steps, added up, will eventually become a huge step toward carrying our Lord's' command to forgive others and to place our trust in him.

Heart to Heart Prayer

Jesus looked up to Heaven and prayed, "O Father most holy, protect them with your name which you have given me [that they may be one, even as we are one.] As long as I was with them, I guarded them with your name which you gave me. I kept careful watch, and not one of them was lost, none but him who was destined to be lost – in fulfillment of Scripture. Now, however, I come to you; I say all this while I am still in the world, that they may share my joy completely. I gave them your word, and the world has hated them for it; they do not belong to the world [any more than I belong to the world.]"... "Consecrate them by means of truth - `Your word is truth.' As You have sent me into the world, so I have sent them into the world; I consecrate myself for their sakes now, that they may be consecrated in truth."

From John 17

Heart to heart prayer...that's how Jesus prayed to the Father in this gospel reading. He spoke to God straight from his heart. As you know, there are many types of prayer, all of them good, but I think heart to heart prayer is critical in developing a personal relationship with Jesus Christ. Talking to God in our own words helps us establish a close, intimate and personal relationship with our Lord.

Where is the best place for heart to heart prayer? It's wherever we feel close to God. For some people, it might be while gardening or exercising; perhaps, it's in a comfortable chair with our eyes closed. Still others might prefer to be in a chapel before the Blessed Sacrament. I often have heart to heart talks with our Lord while I'm driving my truck on the highway with music blaring. For me, another place for heart to heart prayer is at my parents' farm as I'm walking my dog through the woods and fields. Fifty percent of my Sunday homilies come from those prayer

162

experiences. The best place to pray is where we feel in touch with God.

How long should we pray? The length of prayer is not as important as the frequency of prayer. Try to include heart to heart prayer everyday even if it's of short duration. This can be compared to an athlete's finding it more beneficial to train one hour each day, rather than one day per week for several hours.

Try to pray at the same time each day. We are creatures of habit. I find that if I do not pray at the same time each day, the day often comes and goes, seemingly without the opportunity for quality prayer.

What should we bring to God in our heart to heart prayer? We must bring our love, sincerity and openness. We can share our problems, disappointments, frustrations, dilemmas and needs. We should bring the joys of our life as well. Talk to God about all those things. We'll feel God's presence when we talk heart to heart everyday. It's beautiful prayer.

Thanking God

On his journey to Jerusalem Jesus passed along the borders of Samaria and Galilee. As he was entering a village, ten lepers met him. Keeping their distance, they raised their voices and said, "Jesus, Master, have pity on us!" When he saw them, he responded, "Go and show yourselves to the priests." On their way there they were cured. One of them, realizing he had been cured, came back praising God in a loud voice. He threw himself on his face at the feet of Jesus and spoke his praises. This man was a Samaritan.

Jesus took the occasion to say, "Were not all ten made whole? Where are the other nine? Was there no one to return and give thanks to God except this foreigner?" He said to the man, "Stand up and go your way; your faith has been your salvation."

From Luke 17

The heat wave of 1995. Recall that the city of Chicago was especially hard hit with extreme heat in the summer of 1995; some six hundred people died from the heat in that city. I remember reading an article from our local newspaper that revealed that forty-one of the people who died from that heat wave were buried in a mass grave because no one claimed their bodies. No one missed them, no one cared about them. They had no money, family or friends. It's stories like this that stop us in our tracks and we think, thank you God, thank you for everything and for all I take for granted.

The reading above talks about the curing of the lepers. Leprosy was the worst affliction one could have at the time of Jesus. Leprosy was almost always fatal and it was contagious. Lepers were excluded from the community and, sadly, leprosy was believed to be a punishment from God for sin. Therefore, people

164

looked down their noses at lepers. In this parable, Jesus cured ten lepers. What excitement they must have felt after our Lord cured them! Yet only one of the ten came back to thank Jesus for making him well. "Where are the other nine?" asked Jesus, "Where are the other nine?"

About ten years ago, I made an agreement with myself, an agreement I still keep today. When I say my prayers in the morning, I ask God for all my needs and desires, the graces I need to get through the day and I say prayers for those who have asked me to pray for them. At night, however, my prayer is not a prayer of petition; it is a prayer of thanks to God for all the blessings of the day. That little exercise has made me a happier and more contented person because I am much more aware of all that I have and less aware and less concerned with what I don't have. However we choose to do it, let us take time regularly to thank God for his abundant blessings.

The Real Jesus

Now someone approached [Jesus] and said, "Teacher, what good must I do to gain eternal life?" He answered him, "Why do you ask me about the good? There is only One who is good. If you wish to enter into life, keep the Commandments." He asked him, "Which ones?" And Jesus replied, "You shall not kill; you shall not commit adultery, you shall not steal; you shall not bear false witness; honor your father and your mother; and you shall love your neighbor as yourself."

From Matthew 19

I love "make your own sundaes." Given my choice I'd take vanilla ice cream, hot fudge, nuts, whipped cream and a cherry. I'd pass on the butterscotch, fruit, etc. I wish we could "make your own Jesus," but we can't. Some people think we can. For example, in the past several years there has been a significant amount of violence at abortion clinics. Abortion doctors have been shot and killed in Florida and in Buffalo, New York. Many of the individuals or groups responsible for the violence at these clinics claim to be devout Christians and profess to have carried out these acts "in the name of Jesus Christ." But the Jesus they have chosen to worship does not exist. The Jesus of the New Testament said, do not kill, love your enemies and do not judge. The Jesus they have chosen to worship is the Jesus of their dreams.

Granted, it would be nice to be able to "make your own Jesus." Given my choice, I'd like a Jesus who wouldn't ask me to pick up my cross and follow him, a Jesus who wouldn't ask me to forgive and forget, a Jesus who would tell me that the commandments are optional. But that Jesus does not exist. The truth is, if we choose to follow Jesus, we must accept the whole package; we can't pick and choose by "making your own Jesus."

The New Testament clearly outlines who Jesus Christ is, what he has asked us to do in this life and what he promises us in the life to come. This is the Jesus with whom we must fall in love, struggle, and grow.

Complacency

Jesus said to the Pharisees, "Once there was a rich man who dressed in purple and linen and feasted splendidly every day. At his gate lay a beggar named Lazarus who was covered with sores. Lazarus longed to eat the scraps that fell from the rich man's table. The dogs even came and licked his sores. Eventually the beggar died. He was carried by angels to the bosom of Abraham. The rich man likewise died and was buried. From the abode of the dead where he was in torment, he raised his eyes and saw Abraham afar off, and Lazarus resting in his bosom. He called out `Father Abraham, have pity on me.' `My child,' replied Abraham, `remember that you were well off in your lifetime, while Lazarus was in misery. Now he has found consolation here, but you have found torment.'"

From Luke 16

He must have been a pitiful sight. Lazarus, a beggar with sores covering his body, was so helpless that dogs came and licked his sores. Lazarus lived to gather the scraps of bread from the floor that the rich man discarded from his abundant table. What a pitiful sight Lazarus must have been.

But why did God condemn the rich man to a life of torment after his earthly death? The scriptures do not indicate that the rich man physically, mentally or verbally abused Lazarus, he didn't unjustly imprison Lazarus, nor did he force Lazarus to become his slave. Why was the rich man condemned to a life of torment? Because he failed to help the suffering Lazarus when he had the means to do so. The rich man had become so complacent in his lifestyle that he felt no compassion or pain for someone suffering in his midst. He had become blind and numb to the human suffering around him.

There are many Lazarus' in our midst because a Lazarus is anyone who is suffering or in pain. For example, a Lazarus might include those who are lonely, someone who has lost a job, those who suffer from depression or other illnesses, a person who has experienced the loss of a loved one, those who have few friends, a young person caught in the grip of alcohol or drugs, those who cannot afford the basic necessities of life, an individual suffering from unhealthy guilt, people who have low esteem and on and on.

Please God, let us never become so complacent in our lifestyle that we become blind and numb to the Lazarus' around us. If there is pain and suffering in our midst, may it motivate us to do something about it.

The Eucharist

Jesus said to the crowds, "I myself am the living bread come down from Heaven. If anyone eats this bread he shall live forever; the bread I will give is my flesh for the life of the world...He who feeds on my flesh and drinks my blood has life eternal, and I will raise him up on the last day. For my flesh is real food and my blood is real drink. The man who feeds on my flesh and drinks my blood remains in me and I in him. Just as the Father who has life sent me and I have life because of the Father, so the man who feeds on me will have life because of me.

From John 6

How many times will the average Catholic receive communion during the course of his or her lifetime? According to my calculations, about 4,200 times. To come up with that number, I assumed that a person received their First Communion in the second grade, and that they lived into their late seventies. Further, that number assumes that the individual attended Mass weekly, on Holy Days of Obligation and that they attended a couple of funerals and weddings each year. So, the average Catholic will receive the bread of life approximately 4,200 times in their lifetime.

Question: how many of those 4,200 times does the Eucharist make it to our hearts? The Eucharist will probably touch our mouths and stomachs more than four thousand times in our lifetime, but how often will it touch us with true meaning? Here's a litmus test that will help each individual to answer that question for themselves. The more the Eucharist touches our hearts, the more we will find ourselves being kind, compassionate, forgiving, merciful, and loving. The more the Eucharist touches our hearts, the less we will experience things like bitterness, passion, anger, harsh words, slander and malice.

I don't think God cares if we receive the Eucharist 4,200 times in a lifetime or 42,000 times. What God wants to know is, how many times did the Eucharist touch our hearts?

The Love of Money

[Jesus] said to the crowd, "Avoid greed in all its forms. A man may be wealthy, but his possessions do not guarantee him life." He told them a parable in these words: "There was a rich man who had a good harvest. 'What shall I do?' he asked himself. 'I have no place to store my harvest. I know!' he said. 'I will pull down my grain bins and build larger ones. All my grain and my goods will go there. Then I will say to myself, you have blessings in reserve for years to come. Relax! Eat heartily, drink well. Enjoy yourself.' But God said to him, 'You fool! This very night your life shall be required of you. To whom will all this piled-up wealth of yours go?' That is the way it works with the man who grows rich for himself instead of growing rich in the sight of God."

From Luke 12

Lures...lures are things made to look attractive, but ultimately they trick you into something undesirable. Lures attract, tempt and entice.

Some years back we had a problem in the rectory with very small moths; they were everywhere, in every room. So we bought some moth traps. The traps, small boxes lined with a sticky substance on the inside, held a lure to attract the moths. When a moth went for the lure, its wings would come in contact with the sticky substance and it would get caught. The traps eventually solved our problem; however, it was interesting to watch the moths before they entered the trap. The moths would fly around and around the trap for hours before finally going inside it. They seemed to sense danger but, ultimately, they could not resist the lure inside the trap.

Wealth can be a natural lure for humans. Like the moths, we can sense the danger, in this case, the danger associated with the love of money. We know that money can't buy happiness; the

172

two have little to do with each other. We know that money can split apart families and it can cause us to make poor decisions. We know that money has nothing to do with getting to heaven. We sense the danger of the lure of money, yet money attracts us, tempts us, entices us.

In Luke's gospel, chapter 12, God is not telling us that money is bad; indeed, we need it in order to live. However, God *is* telling us that the *love of money* is dangerous and it is a potentially deadly lure.

Speech

Jesus left Tyrian territory and returned by way of Sidon to the Sea of Galilee, into the district of the Ten Cities. Some people brought him a deaf man who had a speech impediment and begged him to lay his hand on him. Jesus took him off by himself and away from the crowd. He put his fingers into the man's ears and spitting, touched his tongue; then he looked up into Heaven and emitted a groan. He said to him, "Ephphatha!" (that is, "Be opened!") At once the man's ears were opened; he was freed from the impediment, and began to speak plainly.

From Mark 7

In 1973, while I was in high school, there was an assembly held to welcome and listen to a guest speaker. The guest speaker was a man who had been a lieutenant in the U.S. Army. He had just been released from a North Vietnamese prison after several years as a prisoner of war. Many of those years involved solitary confinement. I still remember his message as he reflected that day upon his time in solitary confinement. He said, "Never take for granted God's gift of words, the ability to speak and to listen," because, as he said, "you may never know what you have until you no longer have it." I have a feeling that the man whom Jesus healed in the gospel would tell us the same thing...that we should never take the gift of words, of verbal communication, for granted. However, as all of us know, any gift given by God can be misused. The gift of language is no exception. Words can heal, but they also can cut. They can express love, but can also express hate. Words can express compassion, but they also can be used to ridicule.

The gospel challenges us to ask ourselves, "How do we use God's gift of speech?" Do we build up people with our words, and hence, build up the Kingdom of God as the gift was intended, or do we tear people down with our words, and hence, tear down the Kingdom of God?

Being Counter-Cultural

Jesus had to pass through Samaria, and his journey brought him to a Samaritan town named Shechem near the plot of land which Jacob had given to his son, Joseph. This was the site of Jacob's well...When a Samaritan woman came to draw water, Jesus said to her, "Give me a drink." The Samaritan woman said to him, "You are a Jew. How can you ask me, a Samaritan and a woman, for a drink?" "If only you recognized God's gift, and who it is that is asking you for a drink, you would have asked Him instead, and he would have given you living water..." He told her, "Go, call your husband, and then come back here." "I have no husband," replied the woman. "You are right in saying you have no husband!" Jesus exclaimed. "The fact is, you have had five, and the man you are living with now is not your husband..." "Sir," answered the woman, "I can see you are a prophet..." Many Samaritans from that town believed in him on the strength of the woman's testimony.

From John 4

Jesus was crazy, at least that's how many people viewed him. Why? Because he broke all the social rules of the day; he defied the socially accepted norms. Note three things concerning Jesus' encounter with the Samaritan woman at Jacob's well. First, Jesus' encounter at the well was with a woman. At the time of Jesus, men spent little time with women because they were thought to be inferior. When you read the scriptures, you find that Jesus didn't buy into that idea. Rather, Jesus valued women; he talked with them without embarrassment, he defended them, he developed close relationships with women like Martha and Mary, and he performed miracles at the request of women. The concept of women being inferior was absent for Jesus.

176

Second, this woman at the well was not a Jewish woman; she was a Samaritan woman. Jews hated Samaritans more than they hated pagans. The most painful insult for a Jew was to be called a Samaritan. That's why the disciples were shocked to see Jesus conversing with a Samaritan.

Third, the Samaritan woman was a well-known sinner. She had been married five times and was living with a man when she met Jesus. In the Jewish mind, the Messiah would not be spending time with public sinners and social outcasts, but Jesus did. Jesus spent most of his time with humble sinners, and as little time as possible with the self-righteous. Jesus worked outside the envelope. He worked outside the socially accepted norms of his day. That's one reason why he was mocked, laughed at and thought to be crazy.

Jesus loves "crazy" people, people who don't live by society's expectations and norms, but rather, by the expectations and norms of the gospel. Jesus loves people who do crazy things, such as forgiving those who hurt them, loving their enemies, serving one another and giving to the poor. He loves those who pick up their crosses and follow him. Doing such "crazy" things might make us stick out like a sore thumb in society and, like Jesus, we might very well be mocked, laughed at, and thought to be crazy. Maybe that's why Jesus said, "Blessed are you when they insult you and persecute you and utter every kind of evil against you because of me, for your reward will be great in heaven."

177

Overworking

Jesus entered a village where a woman named Martha welcomed him to her home. She had a sister named Mary, who seated herself at the Lord's feet and listened to his words. Martha, who was busy with all the details of hospitality, came to him and said, "Lord, are you not concerned that my sister has left me all alone to do the household tasks? Tell her to help me."

The Lord in reply said to her: "Martha, Martha, you are anxious and upset about many things; one thing only is required. Mary has chosen the better portion and she shall not be deprived of it."

From Luke 10

I read recently that the average American today works ten to fifteen hours more per week than did the average American forty years ago. In other words, we have become more like Martha and less like Mary. In Luke's gospel, Martha is caught up in her work; she is anxious and upset that Mary is not helping her with the details of hospitality. Mary on the other hand, is simply enjoying our Lord's presence; she is not concerned with all the details. Our Lord says to Martha, calm down, relax and enjoy yourself as your sister is doing. Like Martha, we too can get caught up in the details of life, so that we find ourselves running hard all the time.

I believe that dying people can teach us a lot about life. I've never heard a dying person say that they wished they had spent more time in the office or that they'd taken better care of their house. But frequently I do hear them speak about times of pleasure and relaxation spent with family and friends and their regrets that they did not do more of it.

God created us to enjoy life to its fullest, and relaxation and enjoyment are a big part of life. I hope we all take time to smell the roses, to rest, to spend time with family and friends, to enjoy life, because life is too short to be always caught up in details, duties and tasks.

The Immensity of God

Jesus said to his disciples: "I have much to tell you, but you cannot bear it now. When he comes, however, being the spirit of truth he will guide you to all truth. He will not speak on his own, but will speak only what he hears, and will announce to you the things to come. In doing this he will give glory to me, because he will have received from me what he will announce to you. All that the Father has belongs to me. That is why I said that what he will announce to you he will have from me."

From John 16

Recently I've noticed that there are an increasing number of labrador retrievers being used as seeing eye dogs and for police work. I'm told that one of the reasons for this is that labs are viewed as one of the most intelligent of animals. Yet, even the most intelligent animal is not able to understand that 2+2=4; animals simply don't have the capacity to capture that concept. Likewise, the most intelligent human beings will never be able to approach the capacity of God. God extends far beyond the capacity of the human kingdom and that can be frustrating to us because we won't always know why some things happen or how some things can be so. Take, for example, the concept of the Blessed Trinity. The human mind cannot totally understand how one God can be three persons. Some of the greatest minds known to humanity have struggled with the concept of the trinity: Origen, Augustine and Acquinas. They could only scratch the surface of this great mystery; it simply goes beyond our human capacity.

All throughout this life of ours we will run into things that we won't understand; we won't be able to understand why they happened or how they could happen. We have two options for dealing with this. Option 1 is to say, "God, I'm a smart person, so if I can't understand this then there must be something wrong or it must not be so." So when we run into things we can't understand or which have no apparent reason behind them, we can leave the faith. Option 2 is to say, "God, you are bigger than I. My mind is like a glass of water and yours is like the ocean. I can understand some of you but only a small portion of you. God, there are a lot of things that happen in my life that I don't understand but that's o.k. because you're God and I'm not. Someday I'll understand but it won't be in this lifetime. In the meantime, I'm going to live out this faith even though I don't understand why or how some things happen."

It's our choice. We can pick option 1 or option 2.

Death of a Loved One

Jesus said to his disciples:
"Do not let your hearts be troubled.
Have faith in God
and faith in me.
In my Father's house there are many dwelling places;
otherwise, how could I have told you
that I was going to prepare a place for you?
I am indeed going to prepare a place for you,
and then I shall come back to take you with me,
that where I am you also may be."

From John 14

Have you noticed that Jesus never fully defined heaven in the scriptures? Why? Because our vocabulary is incomplete. Any vocabulary is based on human experience and, because we have never experienced heaven, our vocabulary doesn't contain adequate words to describe or define heaven. So, when Jesus tells of heaven, he uses analogies to give us a taste or a feel for what heaven is like.

In John, chapter 14, Jesus tells us heaven is like a big house with many rooms. In that house, God has prepared a room for all of us. God secured that room for us on the day we were baptized and he has been decorating and preparing that room for us ever since, in anticipation of our arrival.

Perhaps you have lost a loved one recently. Have you ever thought about that special room God has prepared for him or her? What will be in that room when you visit your loved one in heaven someday? Will there be a full wine rack, a reclining chair, a fireplace with fresh flowers on the mantle and golf clubs leaning against the wall? Will the view out the window be that of a lake, a mountain, or a tennis court? Which picture of you will be hanging on the wall?

When the death of a loved one touches our lives our hearts are filled with pain. But somewhere in the midst of all that pain we must find joy for our loved one because he or she has finally inherited that special room God has been preparing…a room where we will someday visit our loved one and once again enjoy their company.

John The Baptist

[John the Baptist] said, "I am the `voice of one crying out in the desert, "Make straight the way of the Lord,"' as Isaiah the prophet said. Some Pharisees were also sent. They asked him, "Why then do you baptize if you are not the Messiah or Elijah or the Prophet?" John answered them, "I baptize with water, but there is one among you whom you do not recognize, the one who is coming after me, whose sandal strap I am not worthy to untie."

From John 1

The first chapter of the gospel of John talks about John the Baptist and his role in the plan of salvation. John the Baptist, who announced the coming of Christ, reminds me of a traffic officer. You've seen the traffic officers with the bright orange cones on the end of their flashlights, directing traffic at night. The officers' function is to point people in the right direction. That was one of the functions of John the Baptist; he attempted to get people pointed in the right direction, and to point them towards Christ.

Symbolically speaking, there are a lot of John the Baptists in the world today who help to point us toward Christ by what they say and do. Let me give you two examples of where I encountered a "John the Baptist" in this world.

While I was a seminarian I visited a man who was paralyzed from the neck down and couldn't speak. Bringing this man the Eucharist was a moving experience for me. There was excitement in his eyes and tears when he received the host. This man was a John the Baptist for me; he pointed me in the right direction and helped me to re-focus on Christ.

Second, some years ago, I was at a "journey" retreat with several young adults aged 15 to 18 years. Part of the retreat was a penance service and I had been invited to help with confessions. After about an hour of celebrating the sacrament of reconciliation

184

with those young adults I came out of that building spiritually fired up. Those young people were "John the Baptists" for me; they directed me toward Christ.

My point is simply this: there are contemporary John the Baptists in all of our lives. They may not eat wild honey and grasshoppers, or dress in camel's hair as John the Baptist did, but they do point us toward Christ without even knowing it. All of us are called to be John the Baptists for others through what we say and do.

"Worshipping" Mary

The parents of Jesus used to go every year to Jerusalem for the feast of the Passover, and when he was twelve they went up for the celebration as was their custom. As they were returning at the end of the feast, the child Jesus remained behind unknown to his parents. Thinking he was in the party, they continued their journey for a day, looking for him among their relatives and acquaintances.

Not finding him, they returned to Jerusalem in search of him. On the third day they came upon him in the temple sitting in the midst of the teachers. Listening to them and asking them questions. All who heard him were amazed at his intelligence and his answers.

When his parents saw him they were astonished, and his mother said to him: "Son, why have you done this to us? You see that your father and I have been searching for you in sorrow."" He said to them: "Why did you search for me? Did you not know I had to be in my Father's house?" But they did not grasp what he said to them.

He went down with them then, and came to Nazareth, and was obedient to them. His mother meanwhile kept all these things in memory.

From Luke 2

Recently I was talking to a young couple who lives in the southeastern United States, and they were mentioning how some people in their religion firmly believe that Catholics worship idols, Mary, our Blessed Mother, being one of those "idols." I told them that as Catholics we do not worship Mary because she was a human being; we worship God and God alone. However, Mary has a very special place within our Church and within our hearts because she is the Mother of God. She was the one who taught Jesus how to walk and talk; she was the one who taught him his prayers. The way Jesus loved people and the way that he healed and forgave people says a lot about Mary.

Some people ask of Catholics, "How about all the statues and pictures of Mary; doesn't that constitute idolatry?" Our answer to that is "no," for this reason. In all of our homes, we have pictures of loved ones who have passed away, maybe on top of our televisions or in our bookcases. We don't use these pictures as a means of worshipping our deceased loved ones. Rather, the pictures help to visually remind us of the great love we have for them and the special place that they hold within our hearts. It's the same with the pictures and statues of Mary in our churches and homes. They are visual reminders of our great love for our Blessed Mother.

No, Catholics don't worship Mary, but we do honor her and love her dearly. She is our model; our model in obedience to God and our model as someone who walked by faith, even in times of suffering and uncertainty. She is very, very special to us.

Peak Experiences

As Jesus passed on... two blind men followed [Him], crying out, "Son of David, have pity on us!" When he entered the house, the blind men approached him and Jesus said to them, "Do you believe that I can do this?" "Yes, Lord," they said to him. Then he touched their eyes and said, "Let it be done for you according to your faith." And their eyes were opened.

From Matthew 9

A few years ago, I talked to a man in his late thirties who was going blind. We only had about a fifteen-minute conversation, but he helped me to understand, in a way I had never known, what it was like to be blind. The man helped me to understand how it felt to lose his job because he could no longer carry out his duties. He helped me to understand what it was like to have to enter into assisted living because he could no longer care for himself. He helped me to understand what living in a world of darkness, 24 hours a day, was like. He helped me to understand the fear, the hopelessness, the loss and the exclusion that blindness causes. That fifteen-minute conversation helped me to understand the mindframe of the two blind men in today's gospel. They were desperate men. They had heard stories about Jesus' healing power so they waited for him. When Jesus cured these men of their blindness, it must have brought them pure joy. That encounter with Jesus certainly had been a peak experience for the blind men. No matter how long those two men lived, they never could have forgotten that experience.

You and I have peak experiences as well, special moments with Jesus, just like the two blind men. Let me share with you a peak moment in which I experienced our Lord in a very powerful way. Some years ago I visited a woman who was dying. She was very scared to die. It wasn't until two weeks prior to her death that she was able to talk to me about her fears. I told her that every time she became fearful, to say a simple, repetitive prayer: "Lord, give me the grace to trust that you will take care of me no matter what happens." Five days later I visited this woman again and she was like a different person; she was at peace with her impending death. God had touched her in a deep and meaningful way. The miracle that God performed on her was as real to me as if I were standing next to the two blind men as Jesus restored their sight. When I think back on that dying woman, her miracle brings pure joy to my heart.

You and I have peak experiences with God. They don't happen nearly often enough but they are wonderful experiences. Savor them, relive them, rejoice in them.

Christmas

When the angels had returned to Heaven, the shepherds said to one another, "Let us go over to Bethlehem and see this event which the Lord has made known to us." They went in haste and found Mary and Joseph, and the baby lying in the manger; once they saw, they understood what had been told to them concerning this child. All who heard of it were astonished at the report given them by the shepherds. Mary treasured all these things and reflected on them in her heart. The shepherds returned, glorifying and praising God for all they had heard and seen, in accord with what had been told them.

From Luke 2

I realize that not all of you are football fans, but during a Lions vs. Jets game some years ago, there was a very scary moment. Permit me to outline the setting of the story.

The game was an important one so the fans were really into the moment; they were on their feet; there was emotion, deafening noise...you could feel the adrenaline flowing on the part of both fans and players. Then, in an instant, everything changed when one of the players was hit in the head, suffering trauma to the spinal column. Reggie Brown lay motionless on the field for twenty minutes. Fans slumped back into their seats; players cried, held hands and prayed together. The intensity, emotion and excitement of the game suddenly turned into fear, helplessness and uncertainty.

Isn't that sometimes the case with our lives as well? A sense of fear, helplessness and uncertainty can come upon us in an instant because there are so many things over which we have no control. For example, it could be a parent saying, "We've had to rush your brother to the hospital." Maybe it's a boss saying, "Thanks for the twenty years of service, but we're downsizing and you're not part of our future plans." Maybe it's a doctor saying, "You have cancer." Perhaps it's a call in the middle of the night telling you, "Your daughter has been involved in an automobile accident." Maybe it's a spouse saying, "I want a separation," or the school principal telling you, "Your classmate was accidentally killed last night." Fear, helplessness and uncertainty...we all know the feeling; we all know the void it produces.

When baby Jesus was born into this world, he brought with him the offer of three gifts: stability, hope and inner peace; three gifts that the world cannot offer but Jesus can. That's why this faith of ours is worth living out, worth investing ourselves in. That's why the birth of our savior in a stable in Bethlehem some 2000 years ago is the most significant event the world has ever known and that's why our hearts are filled with pure joy on Christmas.

The Stations of the Cross

On the first day of the week, at dawn, the women came to the tomb bringing the spices they had prepared. They found the stone rolled back from the tomb; but when they entered the tomb, they did not find the body of the Lord Jesus. While they were still at a loss what to think of this, two men in dazzling garments appeared beside them... The men said to them, "Why do you search for the living One among the dead? He is not here; He has been raised up. Remember what He said to you while He was still in Galilee – that the son of man must be delivered into the hands of sinful men, and be crucified, and on the third day rise again."

From Luke 24

Entering into the Stations of the Cross can be a very moving experience. They are the story of Good Friday, the story of the passion and death of our Lord. Upon further reflection, I would say that the Stations sometimes represent the story of our own lives. For example, at the second station, Jesus picks up his cross and begins to carry it. We all carry a cross at times in our lives. The crosses we carry are not wooden crosses but they are just as heavy and burdensome. The crosses we sometimes carry could be things like struggles with our health, a disability or an addiction; they could be job-related crosses or perhaps the cross is that we have no job. Maybe we struggle academically or we don't have many friends. Some of us experience difficulties in our relationships with our children or with our parents. Perhaps we are experiencing the pain of divorce, or find ourselves in a stagnant marriage, or struggle with the pain of being single and wanting to be married. Maybe the cross we carry is having to watch a loved one suffer or perhaps die. That was the case at the fourth station when Jesus met his afflicted mother and Mary saw face to face her suffering son. Sometimes the weight of our earthly crosses becomes so great that we collapse as Jesus did at the third, seventh and ninth stations.

Yes, sometimes the Stations of the Cross are the story of our lives. However, never forget that the cross of Good Friday is always followed by the joy of Easter Sunday. So when life becomes difficult, when our legs are weak because of the heavy crosses that we bear, remember the resurrection... our resurrection made possible by Christ's resurrection.

Holy Week

As the crowd drew near Bethphage and Bethany on the Mount of Olives, close to Jerusalem, Jesus sent off two of his disciples with the instructions: "Go to the village straight ahead of you, and as soon as you enter it you will find tethered there a colt on which no one has ridden. Untie it and bring it back. If anyone says to you, 'Why are you doing that?' say, 'The master needs it but he will send it back here at once'..." They brought the colt to Jesus and threw their cloaks across its back and he sat on it. Many people spread their cloaks on the road, while others spread reeds which they had cut in the fields. Those preceding Him as well as those who followed cried out: "Hosannah! Blessed be he who comes in the name of the Lord!"

From Mark 11

One year as I prepared for Holy Week, the week preceding Easter Sunday, I was reminded of O. Henry's short story which concerned the Irish potato farmer who failed to pay his income tax, and as a result, went to jail. His wife, understandably upset, sent a letter to the man in jail, asking him: "How can we get along without you now? It's almost time to plant the potatoes and there is no way I can plow that field by myself." From jail, the husband wrote his wife back saying: "Don't plow that field; don't you dare touch it! That's where I buried the money." Several days later, the woman wrote back to her husband: "You dummy! Don't you know they read the mail in jail? Yesterday the sheriff, the FBI, and the Internal Revenue Service agents were here digging up that whole field searching for the money. Now what am I supposed to do?" The following week the husband wrote back to her saying, "Now's the time to plant the potatoes. Now's the time."

Holy Week represents the very core of the Catholic faith...the very core. If there has ever been a time to enter into the

194

anxiety and tension of Jesus' passion, the agony and suffering of his death, and the joy and hope of his resurrection, now's the time... now's the time!

Easter

Early in the morning on the first day of the week, while it was still dark, Mary Magdalene came to the tomb. She saw that the stone had been moved away, so she ran off to Simon Peter and the other disciple and told them, "The Lord has been taken from the tomb! We don't know where they have put him!" At that Peter and the other disciple started on their way toward the tomb...He observed the wrappings on the ground and saw the piece of cloth which had covered the head not lying with the wrappings, but rolled up in a place by itself...He saw and believed.

From John 20

I recently read a story about a woman who had contacted her parish priest in order to plan her funeral. The terminally ill woman discussed with him the music she wanted for her funeral Mass, and talked about what scriptures would be read. She showed him the bible and the rosary she wanted buried with her. As a final request, the woman said to the priest, "I want to be laid out in the casket with a fork in my right hand." "Why?' asked the perplexed priest. The woman explained that in all her years of attending church socials and pot luck dinners, she always remembered that when the dishes of the main course were being cleared, someone would inevitably lean over and say, "Keep your fork." She went on to say, "That was my favorite part because I knew something better was coming, cake, pie, or something wonderful and delightful. I want people to see me in my casket with a fork in my hand and I want them to wonder, 'What's with the fork?' Then I want you to tell them, 'Keep your fork, the best is yet to come.'"

The death of a family member or close friend is perhaps life's most painful moment. The pain of separation is so intense because death seems so final, and yet, the message of Easter is that death is not final and separation from our loved ones is only temporary. Because of Jesus' resurrection from the dead about two thousand years ago, death can be seen simply as a doorway that leads us to eternal life and joy in heaven.

As we go through this life and we face the pain of having to say good-bye to loved ones and friends, or we experience the anxiety of having to face our own mortality, remember: "Keep your fork, because the best is yet to come."

Index

198